Games, Ideas and Activities for Primary Drama

Second edition

Michael Theodorou

PEARSON

Harlow, England • London • New York • Boston • San Francisco • Toronto • Sydney
Auckland • Singapore • Hong Kong • Tokyo • Seoul • Taipei • New Delhi
Cape Town • São Paulo • Mexico City • Madrid • Amsterdam • Munich • Paris • Milan

PEARSON EDUCATION LIMITED
Edinburgh Gate
Harlow CM20 2JE
United Kingdom
Tel: +44 (0)1279 623623
Web: www.pearson.com/uk

First published in 2010 (print)
Second edition published 2014 (print and electronic)

ISBN: 978-1-292-00094-7   (print)
      978-1-292-00106-7   (PDF)
      978-1-292-00125-8   (ePub)

British Library Cataloguing-in-Publication Data
A catalogue record for the print edition is available from the British Library

Library of Congress Cataloging-in-Publication Data
Theodorou, Michael.
 Games, ideas and activities for primary drama / Michael Theodorou. -- Second
edition.
  pages cm. -- (Classroom Gems)
 ISBN 978-1-292-00094-7 (Paperback) -- ISBN 978-1-292-00106-7 (PDF) -- ISBN
978-1-292-00125-8 (ePub)
 1. Drama in education. I. Title.
 PN3171.T55 2013
 372.66044--dc23

10 9 8 7 6 5 4 3 2 1
17 16 15 14 13

Print edition typeset in 8.5/12pt News Gothic by 30
Print edition printed and bound in Malaysia, (CTP-VVP)

NOTE THAT ANY PAGE CROSS-REFERENCES REFER TO THE PRINT EDITION

Contents

Part 3
Character

About the author

Michael Theodorou has taught drama in schools and colleges for over thirty years. He started his teaching career in London and subsequently taught in Berkshire, Oxfordshire, Somerset and Gloucestershire. He now works part time as a teacher and drama consultant.

Introduction

This is a book of practical ideas essentially for primary school pupils aged 5–11 but also suitable for Years 7 and 8 in secondary schools.

The book aims to extend physical, vocal and performance skills in Drama and English lessons. It incorporates tried and tested ideas for movement, voice and characterisation.

Practical activities occupy the main body of the page in a 'What to do' section where teachers will be able to 'lift' ideas that are appropriate for the age range they are teaching and put them into immediate action, depending on how long their lesson lasts. Teachers should not feel obliged to follow slavishly but regard the activities as starting points. One of the main purposes of the book is to allow the teacher the freedom to select their own activities to fit into the structure of their lesson timetable.

There are many opportunities for cross-curricular activities in subjects such as Art and DT, English, Mathematics, History, Geography, Music and PE. These cross-curricular links are indicated at the start of each activity.

The language used is simple and direct in order to provide the busy teacher with instant, 'off the shelf' ideas for starting and developing drama sessions for their age group.

The book is divided into three parts:

1. Movement
2. Voice
3. Character.

The movement activities incorporate hundreds of suggestions for solo, pair and group work. There are many opportunities for movement to music with a list of suitable CDs in the Appendix, each on a particular activity that can be enhanced by the use of music.

The activities on voice focus on solo speech, duologue work, the use of accents and dialects and how to project the voice. There are also vocal exercises to sharpen articulation and the use of timing in choral speech. There are suggested exercises on the use of tongue, teeth and lips to improve speech patterns. There are also poems in certain activities that can be used for either Drama or English lessons.

Most activities include improvisation ideas and at the end of most activities there are suggested 'variations' which can be employed.

The character activities are for exploring characterisation, learning performance skills and consolidating everything that has been learnt in Parts 1 and 2.

Additionally, there are dramatised extracts written by the author, available online, that can be used as scripts. These scripts have been created by the author and used successfully as an aid to characterisation. The scripts include scenes from:

Oliver Twist
Great Expectations
A Christmas Carol
The Cuckoo Clock
The Secret Garden
A Midsummer Night's Dream
Goodbye, Mr Chips.

The scripted extracts can be used either for exploring character, performances in class in front of others or, if rehearsed for longer, can be used for speech and drama examinations, festivals or drama competitions. You can find these extracts at the companion website: **www.pearsoned.co.uk/theodorou**

A note from the author regarding the second edition

Despite periodic changes and new trends in education, the teaching of drama remains basically the same.

In this new edition of *Primary Drama* I have kept to the formula used previously and have added about 20 new activities to the book. The new activities extend and compliment those in the first edition.

Michael Theodorou

To all former pupils.

To my wife, Pat

And to Possum, the inspirational cat.

Part 1
Movement

Movement

Movement is magical and, for the young child, is a natural form of expression so I have included many ideas and suggestions for developing this aspect of classroom drama. I have always found that starting with movement is a stimulating way of developing drama sessions. When music is introduced at an early stage children soon learn to respond in a more uninhibited manner. Moving to music – without necessarily being a dancer – develops a sense of rhythm and can lead to control of the body in a disciplined way. Slow motion movement is especially therapeutic and moving in the same way as a partner or a group makes the child more aware of others as well as improving observation and listening powers.

Fingertips

Physical work starts with the importance of hands and fingertips as they can express so much character.

Suitable for

KS1, KS2

Cross-curriculum links

PE, English

Aims

- To achieve flexibility in muscles and joints.
- To communicate character through gesture.
- To use facial expression.

Resources

- An open space

What to do

1. Ask the class to spread out, and put on any fast music to do a quick warm-up session. You can ask them to do the following movements to the music

   - shake the hands from the wrist
   - shake the arms from the elbow
   - shake the arms from the shoulders
   - move the shoulders up and down
   - roll the shoulders backwards and forwards
   - shake hands and fingers and wrists
   - clap your hands in time to the music
   - bend your knees
   - shake your feet

- waggle your hips
- jump up and down
- raise your knees to your chin
- move with short steps forwards
- move with long strides forwards
- dance to the music.

2. Now concentrate on the face and ask them to move their faces (without touching them) in time to the music

- nose
- cheeks
- eyebrows
- mouth.

3. Ask the class to sit in a circle and do the following actions by themselves

- look at one hand
- look at both hands
- look at backs of hands
- look at five fingers
- look at ten fingers
- look at one thumb
- look at both your thumbs
- look at one index finger
- look at both your index fingers
- point at someone to be your partner.

4. In pairs you can ask them to do the following

- touch palms
- touch fingers
- touch one finger
- shake hands
- touch elbows
- touch wrists
- touch shoulders.

5. The pairs should now be asked to express the following with their hands, alternately one at a time, without voice but with facial expression

- come here
- come here immediately

- please come here
- come here, you naughty person
- hello, how nice to see you
- please come in
- go away
- do go away
- please go away
- shove off
- go to the head teacher
- goodbye
- bye
- see you tomorrow
- see you next year
- I salute you.

6. Ask the pairs to think about and rehearse the following using their fingertips especially. Take turns at being a magician and

- put a spell on the other
- put a curse on the other
- cast a thunderbolt down from heaven
- pray for the other
- take care of the other
- think about stealing from the other
- think evil thoughts about the other.

7. Now pairs stand opposite one another at the farthest end of the room. Ask them to use their fingertips to draw their partner towards them against their will. It is a battle of strength between two wills. Pull them in with your fingertips. Take turns in deciding who will 'win'.

8. Tell the children to imagine there is an invisible cord between them and that they are having a tug o'war with their partner.

Variations

- Some of the above exercises will lend themselves to vocalisation and the teacher can decide to ask the children to insert speech or sounds.
- A piece of dramatic mood music will help to enhance the 'battle of wills' (see Appendix for suggestions).
- Use the command 'freeze' from time to time to capture posture.

Mirror Work

In this activity, which is mainly for pair work, the children are asked to act as real persons and as reflections in a mirror, echoing each other's movements. The use of mood music will enhance the effect (see Appendix for suggestions).

Suitable for

KS1, KS2

Cross-curriculum link

English

Aims

- To sharpen observation.
- To listen intently.
- To work in harmony.
- To enhance rhythmic sense.

Resources

- An open space

What to do

1. Put on some slow music and ask the class to move round the room in the following ways
   - walking forwards in slow motion
   - walking and turning in slow motion
   - walking in a dream
   - walking on a strange planet
   - walking in the desert
   - opening a door slowly
   - sitting down slowly

- standing up slowly
- falling over slowly.

2. Repeat the above in pairs with one person echoing the movement of the other as if they are one.

3. In pairs one child is the reflection in a mirror and the other is a real person. Take turns at being the real person and the reflection. Try it in slow motion first

- combing your hair
- cleaning your teeth
- putting on make-up
- putting on your coat
- putting on a scarf
- putting on gloves
- looking at your tongue
- attending to a cut on your face
- taking some medicine
- eating a cream cake.

4. Practise the following actions together in pairs

- swimming the breaststroke
- swimming freestyle
- swimming the butterfly stroke
- swimming backwards
- a slow aerobics exercise
- a fast aerobics exercise
- eating an ice cream
- marching and saluting.

5. Now ask each pair to rehearse and finally show the following to the rest of the class. Again they must work as one

- listening at a door
- opening a door and being horrified
- listening on one side of a wall
- getting a ladder
- climbing up the ladder
- peeping over the wall
- giving a reaction
- smelling something burning

- entering the kitchen
- solving the problem.

6. The above exercises could now be done as improvisations with speech. The pair can be two different people inventing dialogue and responding in their own way.

7. Get them into groups of four and put on some slow mood music. One of the group must be leader and the others reflect the movement of the leader. They can all take turns at being leader. All the movement should be slow motion

- discovering that you have had something stolen
- eating a meal and being sick
- your favourite TV programme has been cancelled
- your mum has sent you to your room for being naughty.

8. Each group of four can now choose one of the scenarios in item 7 and act it out as a piece of normal improvisation in which everyone plays a different part.

Starters (solo)

> This session can be used to start a Drama lesson in a fun way with children following the teacher's short, sharp instructions as quickly and as accurately as possible.

Suitable for

KS1, KS2

Cross-curriculum links

English, PE, Mathematics

Aims

- To generate physical energy.
- To sharpen listening ability.
- To make children more alert.
- To learn the importance of accuracy in movement.
- To improve concentration.

Resources

- Large open space
- Soft shoes or bare feet

What to do

1. Ask the children to spread out so that they are not too close to anyone else.

2. Tell them that they are to use *both hands* in the following activity. Tell them to touch their own

- head
- cheeks
- ears
- nose
- elbows
- knees

- shoulders
- chin

- waist
- stomach.

3. You can either repeat the above instructions more quickly or go on to the next activity, in which you ask the children to use only *one* hand to touch

- the floor
- one foot
- a knee
- an elbow
- stomach

- shoulder
- nose
- chin
- face
- head.

4. The next part of the session demands greater concentration. You should ask the class to carry out the following commands as quickly as possible

- place your index finger on your lips
- place the palms of your hands on your cheeks
- show me the palms of your hands
- show me the back of your hands
- show me the top of your heads
- show me your teeth
- show me your tongue
- open your mouth as wide as you can
- close your mouth.

5. You can make up your own commands if you wish to and mix the above with the shorter commands. The next part of the session requires more moving around the room. Touch

- a wall
- another wall
- the floor
- a window
- a chair
- a door
- another wall.

Variations

- You could introduce adverbs such as 'slowly', 'quickly', 'gently', 'suddenly' in order to create variation in the movement instructions.
- For KS2 pupils you may wish to introduce more mathematical terms in your instructions such as
  - move in a circle shape
  - move in a figure eight
  - move in a square shape
  - move in a rectangle
  - move along an equilateral triangle
  - move along an isosceles triangle.
- Further variation of individual movement could be used by introducing verbal commands such as 'run', 'stagger', 'tiptoe'.
- With item 5 you could make it a competitive game with a winner at the end. The last person to 'touch a wall' (for example) is 'out' and must sit down while the rest continue the game. The game continues until there is one person left.

Starters (pairs)

This session continues the work on moving quickly but this time each child has to work in conjunction with another person.

Suitable for

KS1, KS2

Cross-curriculum link

PE

Aims

- To observe others.
- To listen to others.
- To work in partnership.

Resources

- Large open space
- Soft shoes or bare feet
- No jackets or blazers to be worn

What to do

1. Ask the children to find a partner. If there is an odd person on their own the teacher should join him or her as their partner.

2. One person stands still. The other person, *with one hand only*, must touch their partner's

- head
- shoulder
- back
- foot
- knee
- cheek
- hand
- elbow
- tummy.

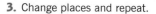

3. Change places and repeat.

4. Now both the children at the same time, *with one hand only*, touch their partner's

- head
- foot
- shoulder
- elbow
- knee
- neck
- hand
- tummy
- back.

5. Now both children at the same time *and with both hands* should touch their partner's

- shoulders
- feet
- head
- back
- elbows
- cheeks
- hands
- knees
- neck.

6. Now both children at the same time *and with one finger only* should touch their partner's

- nose
- foot
- chin
- knee
- elbow
- ear
- shoulder
- head.

7. Now ask the children to do the following together while holding hands

- run and touch a door
- touch a wall
- touch a chair
- touch a window
- sit on the floor
- stand up
- sit on a chair together
- stand up
- sit on the floor
- look up
- look down
- look through a window
- look at your partner
- look at the teacher
- run to the middle of the room.

8. Now ask them to try the following in their pairs. To stand

- back to back
- knee to knee
- side to side
- feet to feet
- head to head
- palm to palm.

Variations

- Once again each of these activities could be enhanced by the use of adverbs such as 'slowly', 'very slowly', 'suddenly', 'smoothly'.
- In item 7 you could create a game by asking each pair to do a series of activities as quickly as possible and the first pair to complete the activities are the winners. For example
  - touch all four walls and then run and sit in the middle of the room
  - touch all the windows in the room and then stand on a chair
  - touch a wall, the floor, another wall, a chair and sit cross-legged
  - touch the teacher, the door, the teacher, the door and stand on one leg in the middle of the room.
- It is always best to vary the pace at which commands are given. You should give commands ranging from very slowly to incredibly fast.

Starters (groups)

> The children will now do movement work in groups of three or four.

Suitable for

KS1 (optional), KS2

Cross-curriculum links

PE, Mathematics

Aims

- To work as a team.
- To observe each other.
- To improve concentration.
- To stimulate alertness.
- To enhance rhythm.

Resources

- An open space
- Soft shoes or bare feet
- No jackets or blazers to be worn
- A CD of military-style music (see Appendix)

What to do

1. Ask them to get into groups of three and stand in a triangle. Ask them to do the following activities

   - point to each other
   - point to the teacher
   - point to a door

- all point at the same door
  - a wall
  - two walls
  - the ceiling
  - a window
  - a light
- point to each other again
- hold hands
- move in a circle
- walk on tiptoe together still holding hands
- look at each other
- sit on the floor still holding hands
- look at the teacher
- move as far away from your partners as possible
- run back to your partners
- get closer together
- stand one metre from your partners
- stand three metres from your partners
- stand with your backs touching your partners' backs
- sit on the floor still touching backs.

2. Still in groups of three ask them to do the following activities

- stand as an equilateral triangle
- stand as an isosceles triangle
- stand as a triangle measuring two metres each side
- stand as a triangle measuring five metres each side
- now make it one metre each side
- move slowly from one metre each side to five metres each side
- move quickly from five metres each side to half a metre each side
- sit and slide from one metre each side to four metres each side
- sit and slide from four metres each side to two metres each side
- still sitting, touch fingertips with your partners
- slowly stand, still touching fingertips
- hands by your sides.

3. Ask them to get into groups of four.

- stand in a square with your partners
- make the square with two-metre sides

- stand in a rectangle
- make the rectangle two metres by four metres
- stand in a circle
- move in a circle
- stand in an oval
- move in an oval shape
- stand side by side facing the same direction
- two face one way, two the other way
- all face in the same direction again
- all move forward one pace at the same time
- all move back one pace at the same time
- move three paces forward at the same time, no speaking allowed
- move three paces back at the same time, no speaking allowed.

4. Now ask them to concentrate on the following, keeping together as much as possible and not speaking to each other

- all face the same direction
- tiptoe forwards together
- turn and tiptoe back to where you started
- tiptoe around the edge of the room, keeping together
- turn and tiptoe back again, making no noise at all
- stand facing the same direction
- stand stiffly to attention
- relax
- stand stiffly to attention again
- all march forward four paces at the same time
- about turn and march back again
- march around the room, keeping together.

5. To the military-style music ask them to undertake the following

- march in pairs around the edge of the room
- turn every eight paces and go in a different direction together
- join your group of four and try the same thing.

Variations

- As the commands become more challenging ask pairs, trios and quartets to operate one group at a time with everyone else watching. The teacher can then give a 'prize' to the group with the best teamwork.
- The command 'freeze' can always be used for any of the above activities.
- In the military-style marching sequence you could experiment with saluting, either one at a time or all together.
- One of the children could be of a higher rank than the others, which will give a reason for saluting.
- The mathematical terms should be explained if children do not understand them.

Moving Through Space

> In this movement activity we experiment with ways in which the body can move both in space and time.

Suitable for

KS1, KS2

Cross-curriculum links

Music, PE

Aims

- To coordinate movement.
- To use your visual imagination.
- To improve your timing.

Resources

- An open space
- Slow music

What to do

1. Put on some slow music and ask the children to stand in a space by themselves and

   - close eyes tight shut
   - open eyes
   - close eyes gently
   - sway to the music keeping feet firmly on the ground
   - sway as if you are the branches of a tree
   - sway as if there is a strong wind
   - sway as if there is a very gentle breeze blowing through you
   - slowly sink down onto the floor and lie down

- slowly open eyes
- breathe in
- breathe out
- breathe in again
- breathe out again
- slowly stand
- look around you
- you are in a strange landscape
- you are on the moon
- you can only move at half your speed
- take five steps in slow motion
- turn and move ten steps in slow motion
- turn slowly and move in circles
- slow down even more
- the faster you want to move the slower you go
- breathe slowly and gently sink to the ground
- when you hear me clap, you wake up!

2. Ask the children to find a partner and imagine they are astronauts on the moon. They are wearing spacesuits and can only move in slow motion as follows

- move together in slow motion
- you both see a strange rock on the ground
- you kneel down to examine it
- you pick it up and look at it
- the rock grows bigger and bigger
- then it grows smaller and smaller
- then it disappears
- you look for it
- you see another rock further off
- you move towards it and examine it
- it grows bigger and bigger
- then it grows smaller and smaller
- it disappears again
- you look for it again
- you suddenly see a huge rock rolling towards you
- you run as fast as you can to get to your spaceship
- the rock is catching up on you
- it will crush you.

3. Divide the class into slow movers and fast movers.

- the fast movers all walk together across the room twice
- the slow movers walk across the room once.

They must all finish at the same time. Try it again, but this time

- the fast movers cross the room four times
- the slow movers twice.

Again, they must all aim to finish at exactly the same time. Increase the number of times as necessary.

4. Try the following game using the idea of half the class as fast movers and half the class as slow movers, with

- the fast movers to raise their arms above their heads six times
- the slow movers three times
- the fast movers to raise their arms twelve times
- the slow movers six times.

They must always aim to finish at exactly the same time with their arms up in the air.

Variations

You could try the following variations of movement if appropriate for the space you have

- moving backwards
- moving sideways.

Fun Games

Here are some suggested games to stimulate the class at the beginning of a session.

Suitable for

KS1, KS2

Cross-curriculum links

PE, English

Aims

- To think quickly.
- To listen carefully.
- To respond to the sound and meaning of words.

Resources

- An open space

What to do

Imaginary Ball

1. Ask the children to stand in a circle to play the game 'Imaginary Ball'.

2. Explain that in this game an imaginary ball, the size of a tennis ball, is thrown across the circle from one person to another.

3. The person throwing the ball must say the name of the person they are throwing to and then throw it immediately. The person who receives the ball must throw it immediately to someone else, saying that person's name.

4. If anyone hesitates or says the wrong name then that person is 'out' and must sit down in the circle.

5. The game continues until there is only one person left, who is the winner.

Bing Bong

1. Explain to the children that in this game they must stand in a circle as above.

2. The teacher chooses a person to start. That person says 'Bing'.

3. The next person in the circle says 'Bong'. The next person in the circle says their OWN name. The next person in the circle says 'Bing'. The next person in the circle says 'Bong'. The next person in the circle says their OWN name. And so on round the circle.

4. If anyone hesitates or says the wrong word, they are 'out' and must sit down.

5. The game continues until there is only one person left, who is the winner.

Hee Haw

1. Tell the children to stand in a circle as above.

2. The teacher chooses a person to start. That person says 'Hee', imitating a donkey.

3. The next person says 'Haw', imitating a donkey. The next person says their OWN name. And so on, round the circle as above.

4. Any one who hesitates or says the wrong word (or laughs) is 'out' and must sit down.

5. The game continues until there is only one person left, who is the winner.

King Kong

1. Ask them to stand in a circle as before.

2. In this game of 'King Kong' the children have to speak in a commanding voice when they utter the words 'King' and 'Kong'. If they have knowledge of the film about the giant ape then they can also imitate a strong movement to go with the voice.

3. The teacher chooses a person to start. That person says 'King' in a booming or commanding voice.

4. The next person says 'Kong' in a booming or commanding voice. The next person says their OWN name in a normal voice. And so on, round the circle.

5. If anyone hesitates, or says the wrong word (or laughs) they are 'out' and must sit down.

6. The game must go as quickly as possible with no hesitation until someone makes a mistake and is 'out'. The last person left is the winner.

Variations

- Variations on the above words could be
  - drip drop (water)
  - plink plonk (piano)
  - clip clop (horse)
  - ding dong (bell).
- Movement and gesture should be encouraged to express the sound of the words.

Circle Work

In this session the class will work mainly in a circle shape and follow the movement of others as well as creating their own pattern of movement.

Suitable for

KS1, KS2

Cross-curriculum link

PE

Aims

- To watch carefully.
- To focus on details.
- To invent original moves.
- To listen to others.

Resources

- An open space

What to do

1. Ask the class to get into a circle shape by touching fingertips with each other. Do a little warm up, which can include the following

   - running on the spot as fast as you can
   - bending the knees and jumping as high as you can
   - feet stuck to the ground and reaching up as far as you can
   - touching your toes ten times
   - walking on the spot in slow motion
   - walking slower and slower until you stop.

2. Ask the group to look at each other and make sure they can see everyone in the circle. Each person in the circle, one at a time, must now make a short facial movement and everyone else in the circle must repeat it.

3. Each person in the circle, one at a time, now makes a movement with their hands and the circle repeats the movement.

4. Each person in the circle, one at a time, now makes a movement with their feet and everyone else repeats it.

5. Each person in the circle, one at a time, now makes a short, sharp 'kung fu' movement and everyone in the circle repeats it. This can be accompanied by an appropriately aggressive sound.

6. Each person in the circle, one at a time, now claps rhythmically and the circle joins in until the next person starts a new rhythm and so on.

7. Each person in the circle, one at a time, stamps a rhythm with their feet and the whole circle repeats it.

Variations

- Once they get used to following each other's movements you can make the procedure more complicated by suggesting the idea of mixing movements and sounds, for example
  - stamping and clapping
  - stamping with one foot and slapping your thigh
  - tapping your head and slapping your cheeks
  - animal movements and sounds.

Object Shapes (pairs)

In this activity children create everyday object shapes with their bodies and give them a personality.

Suitable for

KS1, KS2

Cross-curriculum links

PE, Mathematics, English

Aims

- To gain physical control.
- To use visual imagination.
- To work with others.

Resources

- An open space

What to do

1. Ask the class to spread out and try the following poses one at a time
   - up straight
   - stiffen arms by your side
   - bow your head
   - elbows on knees
   - hands on cheeks
   - hands on waist
   - fists on waist
   - arms in an arch over head
   - one arm up in the air the other on waist
   - go down on your knees with hands on the floor

- hands on the back of the neck
- hands clasped behind back
- on the floor with knees up to chin.

2. Once the children have got used to making odd shapes with their bodies you can start to call out objects and ask them to try to make the following object shapes with their bodies

- a vase
- a bucket
- a pencil
- a table
- a clock
- a table lamp
- a bookcase
- a cannon ball
- a teapot.

3. Now ask them to use their bodies to create the following aspects of nature

- a tree with no leaves – in winter
- a tree with leaves – in hot summer sun
- a tree gently swaying in the breeze
- a tree in a storm
- a very tall tree
- a small bush
- a pretty flower
- a spiky cactus.

4. Now ask them to get into pairs and create the following pairs of objects

- a dustpan and brush
- a salt pot and a pepper pot
- a knife and fork
- a toothbrush and toothpaste
- a cup and saucer
- a pair of trainers
- a pair of vases
- a pair of statues.

5. Still in their pairs ask them to create the following objects with their bodies and give them movement and sound

- a pair of mechanical dolls
- a pair of toy robots
- a pair of toy soldiers
- a cuckoo clock.

6. Ask them to think in terms of a machine, any machine, and give them the following exercises before they create their own personal machines in pairs. Repeat the following movements together

- walk on the spot counting one and two
- walk on the spot counting one and two and three and four
- raise shoulders up and down
- open and close hands
- bow and stand up straight again
- bend the knees and up again
- bend arms from the elbows
- bend hands from the wrist
- open and close all fingers
- raise arms above heads and down again
- step forwards and back again.

7. Now ask them to create together their own machine with appropriate sound effects. If they have difficulty suggest the following

- a machine that wraps up sweets
- a machine that puts corks in bottles
- a machine that produces sausages
- a machine that drives a train.

Object Shapes (groups) (The Fridge)

In this activity children continue working on making up shapes of objects, but this time in larger groups.

Suitable for

KS1 (optional), KS2

Cross-curriculum links

PE, English

Aims

- To work as a team.
- To listen to the ideas of others.
- To experiment with sounds.

Resources

- An open space

What to do

1. Get the class into groups of four. Before starting the rehearsal process ask them to do the following movement exercises as a continuous sequence in their groups

   - all move one step forward together
   - turn right together
   - turn left together
   - move two steps forwards together
   - move two steps back together.

2. Now ask each group to think up their own continuous group movement and move in unison.

3. In groups of three or four they must create objects or foodstuffs in a fridge. Each pupil can choose their own objects but you could give them the following examples

- a pint of milk
- a bottle of beer
- a carton of orange juice
- a bottle of champagne.

Ask them to practise the physical shape of their chosen object and invent a movement, as if they are being used by a human.

4. Try to get them to invent related objects. For example

- a large tomato
- a cucumber
- a stick of celery
- a beetroot.

Ask them to crowd together into the same compartment of the fridge.

5. When they have established a definite set of objects you can start to practise movement. Ask them to imagine that the objects can move, but first of all they must have

- legs
- arms
- a face.

6. You should have a session in which each group concentrates on the individual movement of its fruits or vegetables or bottles.

7. The movement and shape of the objects is important. Give them an adjective that will help them to establish a movement for their object. For example

- a fat tomato
- an angry beetroot
- a thick cucumber
- a thin piece of celery.

8. Another way of establishing the reality of the objects is to have a session in which the items are taken out of the fridge by a human and put back again. When they are put back in they are different

- half a tomato
- beer that has been partially drunk
- cucumber that has been sliced
- celery that has been bitten
- milk that has been left out of the fridge for too long

- beetroot that has been chewed
- champagne that is missing its top and losing its fizz.

9. Another useful set of objects for the fridge that could be rehearsed as above are

- a pot of jam
- a jar of mustard
- a tin of baked beans
- a packet of peas.

Variations

- Objects can move in different ways – try suggesting the following
  - heavily
  - smartly
  - drunkenly
  - beautifully
  - haughtily
  - softly
  - stately
  - commonly.

Objects Shapes (groups)

Now that the children have done a variety of objects they can go straight into creating the shapes and sounds of everyday household machinery that will be familiar to them.

Suitable for

KS1, KS2

Cross-curriculum link

English

Aims

- To work as a team.
- To learn about rhythm.
- To watch and listen.

Resources

- An open space
- A notebook

What to do

1. Get them into groups of four or five at the most. Ask them in their groups to think about and create the shape of the following

- a washing machine
- a food mixer
- a dishwasher
- a tumble dryer.

2. Each group must now work together on the *sound* that is made by the machine in order to make it as real as possible.

3. Once the machine is in perfect working order and the children are happy with the sound and shape of their machine you could suggest the following

- the washing machine makes a funny sound
- the food mixer starts to slow down
- the dishwasher starts to growl
- the tumble dryer starts to smell.

4. Now ask them to try another set of machines used around the house and to form the shape together along with appropriate sounds

- a vacuum cleaner with attachments
- a hairdryer
- an alarm clock
- a television set.

5. As a continuation of this type of work you could ask them to try to think up a 'voice' to go with the object they have created. You could ask them to write a 'monologue' for each of their objects in which they describe

- who they are
- what they look like
- the function they serve
- where they are kept
- who owns them
- how they are used.

6. Split the class into two large groups. Tell them they are going to create a steam engine (and compartments) with sound effects. In order to help them you could suggest they practise the following ideas first. Each member of the group is given a number and each number is given a pose to adopt

- standing
- kneeling
- lying on your side
- lying on your front
- lying on your back
- on all fours
- sitting on the floor
- sitting on a chair
- standing with arms above head
- standing with arms on someone else's shoulders.

7. The steam engine should start slowly and the following could be suggested as movement ideas

- pulling out of the station
- moving at a regular speed
- stopping at a signal
- moving uphill
- pulling into a station
- emergency stop.

8. Some of the children could be passengers getting on and off the train so that the following objects could be created as well

- a sliding door between compartments
- a seat
- a train door
- luggage.

Variations

- A really good group should be encouraged to invent their own machine and use the whole class.
- Key words for the sounds of machines should be used, such as
  - humming
  - growling
  - swishing
  - rattling.

Robots

> In this session we invent games and activities involving robots and mechanical objects.

Suitable for

KS1, KS2

Cross-curriculum links

Science, PE

Aims

- To listen.
- To watch.
- To communicate.
- To speak clearly.

Resources

- An open space
- Some chairs
- Blindfolds

What to do

1. In pairs, one of the children is the master, the other is the robot. The robot is blind and either closes its eyes or has to have a blindfold. The robot must be guided by its master's voice with words such as 'forward', 'left', 'right', 'stop'. The purpose of the game is for the masters to guide their robots through a narrow gap between two chairs at the other end of the room. The teacher decides where the starting line is to be, the position of the chairs at the other end, and

   - asks the children to choose a partner
   - asks them to decide who is going to be master and robot

- gets them to practise giving commands such as 'start' or 'stop'
- reminds the masters to give very definite instructions to their robots
- reminds robots to listen very carefully to their masters and to trust them!

2. Another rule that can be introduced is that the masters must have their backs against a wall at the back while calling instructions to their robots. If they do not, they are disqualified.

3. Two pairs of children can compete to get their robots through the gap in the chairs at the other end of the room. However, if the robots bump into each other by accident then both pairs are out/disqualified. Then another pair of children is chosen to have a go. The children will quickly realise that the only way to get their robots through the chairs without colliding is to give precise instructions.

4. The rules of the game can be varied by the teacher saying that the winner will be the person whose robot comes back and touches the master.

5. In order to make it harder for them further rules could be introduced later in the session or on another day, such as

- if a robot touches a chair the team is disqualified
- if a robot bumps into a wall the team is disqualified.

6. A suitable piece of electronic music such as the theme from *Doctor Who* can be used for atmosphere.

Variations

- Depending on the size of the class, you can have a knockout competition between three pairs with the winner going forward to the next round.
- If you decide on this method, it is useful to have 'twisters' to turn the robots round and round in order to disorientate them before the competition starts.
- You can have two pairs of chairs through which the robots must pass.

Letters and Words

In this activity the children form letters with their bodies and learn to make up words with their bodies.

Suitable for

KS1, KS2

Cross-curriculum links

English, Art

Aims

- To shape letters with the body.
- To shape words with the body.
- To spell.
- To differentiate between vowels and consonants.
- To work as a group.

Resources

- A notebook and pen/pencil
- Drawing paper
- Coloured pencils
- An open space for movement

What to do

1. Ask the class to spread out and do the following as individuals

   - form the letter X with their bodies
   - now do it lying on the floor
   - the letter Y, standing up
   - the same letter, lying down on the floor.

- the letter I standing up
- the same letter, lying on the floor.

You can go through the whole alphabet in this way, if you want to continue.

2. Now ask them to get into pairs and form the following letters together, either standing up or lying on the floor

B D E L O P T U V

3. Ask them to get into groups of three and form the following letters

B F H K N S Y Z

4. Now ask them to get into groups of four and form the following

A C E J L M O P Q R S T W X

5. Now back into groups of two again and form the following words together, either standing up or lying down on the floor

TO   BY   AT   IN   DO   OR

6. Now in groups of three form the following words

CAT   DOG   MAN   PIG   TOP   WAR   ZIP

7. Now in groups of four, as fast as they can, form the following words together, either in small letters or capital letters, lying down or standing up

BANG   KING   FOOL   MIME   WIPE   ZULU

Variations

- The lesson could start with them sitting at their desks and using their notebooks to draw letters both in capitals and small letters.
- Ask them to choose a letter (which could have a face) and then draw it and colour it in.
- Ask them to draw the five vowels (a, e, i, o, u) and then pronounce them, opening their mouths as wide as they can.

- Ask them to write down the following consonants and then use their tongue, teeth and lips to say them

  B, P, M
  D, J, N, S, T
  F, R, V, Y
  K, L, Q, V.

More Letters and Words

> We continue to work on the shapes of letters and more complex sentences, using group movement.

Suitable for

KS1, KS2

Cross-curriculum link

English

Aims

- To work closely with others.
- To stimulate the visual imagination.

Resources

- An open space

What to do

1. In groups of four ask the children to try, as quickly as they can, to form the following sentence by creating the shapes of the letters, either standing up or on the ground

    There is a Green Hill Far Away
    Ding Dong Merrily on High
    Silent Night Holy Night
    In the Deep Mid Winter
    Hark the Herald Angels Sing

    Each word must be shown to you, the teacher, before they go on to the next word. You will decide if they have successfully communicated the word through their shapes.

2. Ask them to get into groups of six and to think of a *group movement* for the following words

   follow
   storm clouds
   horses galloping
   waves rising.

   You must see each group and decide which is the most successful before moving on.

3. Now ask them to repeat with appropriate sounds. You decide which group is the most successful, as above.

4. Now ask them to form a still picture of the above. Again, you decide which group is the most successful.

5. Ask them to form a still picture that bursts into life and then is still again. The same procedure is followed to judge 'success'.

6. Ask each group of six to form the names of each person in the group.

Numbers

This is an activity in which numbers are formed by using different parts of the body.

Suitable for

KS1, KS2

Cross-curriculum link

Mathematics

Aims

- To work with others quickly.
- To work out sums mentally.
- To stimulate the visual imagination.

Resources

- Paper and pencil
- An open space
- A whiteboard

What to do

1. To start the lesson in an energised fashion you can ask the whole class to spread out and show you with their bodies the numbers 1–10. First they can be standing up and then the second time lying on the floor. Call out the numbers fairly quickly.

2. Ask the class to find a partner and create the following numbers together, either by standing up or lying down on the floor

   3   5   7   9   29   98   40   61

3. Ask the pairs to show you, not tell you, the number result from the following sums

- 8 plus 3
- 14 plus 11
- 29 plus 32
- 88 plus 11
- 5 times 6
- 12 times 5

- 4 times 20
- 13 times 4
- 9 plus 17 minus 6
- 3 plus 38 minus 15
- 16 plus 12 minus 2
- 97 plus 13 minus 56.

The first pair to show you the correct number are the winners.

4. Make up a group of four and this time give them the following sums to demonstrate and give the answer

- 4 plus 9
- 2 plus 9
- 3 plus 8
- 5 times 5

- 7 times 3
- 4 times 8
- 5 times 9.

5. Now get them back into pairs and ask them to make the following numbers together

- their age
- their ages combined
- their mother's age
- their father's age
- their birthday
- the number of their house
- how many brothers they have
- how many sisters they have
- the total number of brothers and sisters.

Variations

- The written exercises can start at their desks to get them used to doing sums and then they can move over to the open space.
- You can either write up the sums on the whiteboard or call them out, depending on the mathematical ability of the group being taught.

Leading with the Nose (part 1)

In the following activities children are shown that leading with particular parts of the body can lead to character acting.

Suitable for

KS1 (optional), KS2

Cross-curriculum link

PE

Aims

- To link movement with voice.
- To exaggerate movement.
- To find the right voice for a character.

Resources

- An open space

What to do

1. Ask the class to walk around the space in the following manner
   - walking with your nose forward
   - walking with your stomach sticking out
   - walking with your knees leading
   - walking with your chest leading.

2. Now ask them to do exactly the same but this time saying 'hello' or 'good morning' to others as they pass by.

3. Ask them to get into groups of four and concentrate on the movement of 'leading with the nose'. What kind of voice best suits the action?

4. Ask them in their groups to walk with their stomachs sticking out. What kind of voice best suits the action?

5. Now they must walk in their group with their knees leading. What kind of voice best suits the action?

6. Finally ask them to walk with their chests sticking out and find a suitable voice for the action.

7. Now ask the groups to choose any of the above movements and develop a situation in which a conversation takes place between them, using appropriate voices. You can suggest the following starting lines

- I can smell something nasty (noses)
- What did you have for tea? (stomach)
- Guess what I just heard? (knees)
- Who did you beat up today? (chest)

8. It might be helpful to give them a piece of script from the website in order to try the voices and the movement with a script. I would suggest the following extracts from *A Christmas Carol* as being suitable

- The drunks' scene (stomachs)
- The merchants' scene (noses)
- The laundress scene (knees).

Variations

- As they are exploring the movement you could ask them to do it in slow and fast motion.
- In the improvised conversations (item 7) you could mix up the movements and ask them to have one person using the nose, another the stomach, etc.

Leading with the Nose (part 2)

Once the children have learnt to move leading with different parts of the body the following ideas could be used for further development.

Suitable for

KS1 (optional), KS2

Cross-curriculum link

PE

Aims

- To show physical flexibility.
- To link movement to character.

Resources

- An open space
- Props can be used to help characterise movement, such as walking sticks, false noses, bobble hats, cushions under shirts

What to do

1. Ask the class to do the following movements slowly
   - bend down from the waist until your nose is well forward
   - the same with hands behind your back
   - the same with a sneering expression on your face
   - the same but this time say something.
2. The following could also be attempted slowly
   - bend slowly backwards until your tummy is sticking out
   - the same but put your hands on your tummy

- the same but puff out your cheeks
- the same but say something.

3. Try the following in the same way

- walk forward until your knees are ahead of your body
- the same but put your thumbs in your belts
- the same but with a big grin on your face
- the same but this time say something.

4. The final one, using the chest

- walk forward with your chest leading
- the same but rolling your shoulders
- the same but with an evil expression on your face
- the same but this time speak.

5. Ask them to get into groups of three or four and this time give them a background location in which the action can take place

- a posh restaurant (noses)
- a McDonald's (tummy)
- a hospital (knees)
- a gym (chest).

6. This time tell them that they should include the following expressions in their dialogue

- I say, I say, I say (noses)
- O yum (tummy)
- My knees hurt (knees)
- Look at my muscles (chest).

7. Using some props to help exaggerate the movement you can suggest the following scenarios that the children can develop, making up their own dialogue

- A rich man helps a beggar by giving her/him some money.
- The beggar goes to a café and is served by a very fat waiter. The beggar spends all his money on a fantastic meal.
- The fat waiter's boss tells him he must go on a diet or he'll be sacked because he puts customers off.
- A week later the rich man sees the beggar who is starving because he has spent all his money.

- The rich man takes the beggar to the restaurant where they are served by the fat waiter.
- The boss wants to chuck out the beggar but the rich man stands up for him.
- The fat waiter also stands up for the beggar and the boss sacks him.
- The rich man offers to buy the restaurant. The boss throws them all out.
- The rich man, the beggar and the fat waiter plan their revenge.
- What do they do?

Changing Direction

This activity is about moving to music, rhythm and changing direction. Fast aerobic music is perfect for these movements. Some suggestions are available in the Appendix.

Suitable for

KS1, KS2

Cross-curriculum link

PE

Aims

- To improve physical coordination.
- To watch others.

Resources

- A large open space
- A CD of aerobic music

What to do

1. Put on some fast aerobic-style music and ask the children to move quickly in any way they like in time to the music. Then specify
   - short steps
   - very short steps
   - long steps
   - like a penguin
   - swaying from side to side
   - sideways
   - backwards.

2. Ask them to find a partner and move in exactly the same way as their partner. Go through all the above variations working in pairs.

3. Now the pairs stand still but have to move various parts of the body in time to the music

- arms
- shoulders
- wrists and hands
- fingers
- heads

- waist
- bums
- knees
- all parts of the body.

4. Now they choose the pair nearest to them and make up a group of four. Repeat the variations above and then ask the groups to move together as in item 1. Use the music.

5. Ask the groups to sit down around the edge of the room. Put on the music again and say you will call out instructions for changing direction. Each time you call out an instruction the group must change direction but still remain in rhythm. Do only one group at a time while everybody else watches from the side. Give the following instructions:

- forward short steps
- left
- right
- stop
- forward like penguins
- turn right
- turn left

- forward long steps
- left
- right
- hopping on both feet forward
- left
- right
- stop.

6. Do the same changing direction exercises as in item 5 but with pairs.

7. Divide the class into two and have a team A and a team B. Give each person in the teams a number. Both teams stand at one end of the room. When the music starts number 1s move in a specified way to an opposite wall and then back again and number 2s take over, etc. The winning team will be the one whose members all move in the specified way and finish ahead of their rivals. You can give the teams the following specific ways of moving

- on tiptoe
- very short steps
- very long strides
- like penguins

- hopping on one foot
- hopping on both feet
- moving on all fours.

If a member of a team moves in an inappropriate manner then the team is either disqualified or marks are taken off.

Variations

- You could make the game in item 7 more complicated by saying that each person in the team has to move in a different way, for example 1s walk, 2s run, 3s hop, etc.

Monsters

In the next three activities children are given the opportunity to explore the movement of extraordinary characters from other worlds and exaggerated characters from this world.

Suitable for

KS1, KS2

Cross-curriculum link

PE

Aims

- To stimulate the imagination.
- To show belief in character.
- To practise movement leading to voice.

Resources

- An open space
- Soft shoes or bare feet

What to do

1. As an introduction to these types of characters ask them to move as individuals in the following ways

   - in slow motion, moving the knees as high as they can
   - very short fast steps forwards
   - moving sideways quickly
   - moving slowly with arms outstretched
   - moving slowly bending as low as they can
   - moving up and down slowly as tall as they can.

2. Now ask them to repeat the above movements with suitable facial expressions.

3. Now ask them to repeat the above movements, making continuous sounds as they move.

4. Get them into pairs and repeat the above movements in unison, keeping together as far as possible.

5. Ask them in their pairs to add facial expressions and sounds to their movements.

6. Each pair selects one movement and performs in front of the whole group.

7. Get them into groups of four and ask them to work on the movement and sounds of the following ideas
   - alien creatures on a planet with little gravity
   - creatures from a planet where the light is always bright
   - creatures on a planet where there is no light
   - creatures from a planet where an enemy waits round every corner
   - creatures who dominate a planet.

8. As a final step you should ask the groups to select their best scenario and perform it in front of the whole class.

Variations

- As an alternative starter to the lesson you could put on the music to Bartok's 'Miraculous Mandarin Suite' (Episode 12) and ask them to move to the music as
  - witches
  - devils
  - flying demons
  - any evil character from *Harry Potter*.

More Monsters

This activity continues the work on exaggerated characters and experimenting with movement to suit unreal situations.

Suitable for

KS1, KS2

Cross·curriculum link

English

Aims

- To show suspension of disbelief.
- To communicate with others.

Resources

- Shell suits
- Motorbike helmets

What to do

1. Ask the class as individuals to experiment with making sounds as follows
   - a giant laughing
   - a devil grinning and laughing
   - a witch cackling
   - a magician casting spells
   - a god venting destruction on the world.

2. Now as individuals ask them to add movement to the above characters.

3. Sit the class in a circle and ask each person one at a time to show the rest of the class their version of the above.

4. As pairs ask them to do the following movements together

- walking on glass
- skating on ice
- opening the doors of a spaceship on a strange planet
- exploring a rocky surface
- walking through a hot desert.

5. Now ask each pair to join another pair for some slow motion movement on an alien planet. One pair are aliens, the other pair are astronauts who have just landed. There is no gravity on this planet, everyone has to move very slowly

- scene 1: the astronauts open the door of their spaceship
- scene 2: the alien creatures lie in wait
- scene 3: the astronauts step out and start walking
- scene 4: the alien creatures hide behind a wall
- scene 5: the astronauts suspect there is someone behind the wall
- scene 6: the aliens sniff the air
- scene 7: the astronauts approach the wall and listen
- scene 8: the alien creatures also listen on the other side of the wall
- scene 9: the astronauts touch the wall
- scene 10: the aliens make a sound
- scene 11: the astronauts hear the sound and are scared
- scene 12: the aliens bury themselves in the earth
- scene 13: the astronauts take out their laser guns
- scene 14: the astronauts come round the wall slowly
- scene 15: the astronauts see nothing
- scene 16: the aliens leap up out of the earth making loud sounds
- scene 17: the astronauts drop their guns and run back to their spaceship
- scene 18: the aliens pursue them
- scene 19: the astronauts close the door of the spaceship
- scene 20: the aliens are shut out
- scene 21: the spaceship takes off.

6. Once they have rehearsed the above sequence for a while, ask each group to perform the whole scenario in front of the class.

A suitable piece of music could be played during the entire sequence. See Appendix for suggestions.

7. Create your own written alien language by using either symbols or words. As a part of your English lessons ask the class to compose logs, written by aliens, in which they recount the landing of the astronauts on their planet.

8. In a similar way a log entry by the astronauts could be attempted in English lessons, using more conventional language!

Variations

- You can suggest the following ideas to make their movements as strange as possible but they must believe in what they are doing
  - the aliens can see with the palms of their hands
  - the aliens can see with their ears
  - the astronauts wear shell suits and helmets
  - the aliens are stuck together.

Even More Monsters

In this activity we focus on movement and voice for more traditional characters from popular culture.

Suitable for

KS1, KS2

Cross-curriculum link

English

Aims

- To use appropriate accents for a role.
- To show imitation of a style of acting.

Resources

- Black cloak for Dracula
- Props such as pirates' hats

What to do

1. Ask them to try the following facial expressions as a starter for experimenting with monster movement

   - make an ugly face
   - make an ugly sound
   - twist your mouth
   - make a sound with your twisted mouth
   - make your eyes stare
   - narrow your eyes
   - mime eating in a disgusting way
   - move and chatter like an ape.

2. Continue to experiment vocally in the following ways while moving

- a deep growl
- a wolf howling
- a monster dog barking
- a giant breathing
- an animal sniffing
- a vampire getting angry.

3. Now ask them to say the following in whatever voice/accent and with whatever movements they think appropriate

> Fi, fi, fo, fum, I smell the blood of an Englishman
>
> Be he alive or be he dead
>
> I'll grind his bones to make my bread.

If appropriate ask each person in the group to act this out in front of the rest of the class and the most frightening performance wins a prize.

4. Do the same with the following speech

> You think to destroy me!
>
> Me who has been alive for centuries!!
>
> You fools!!!

As above have a competition for the fiercest interpretation.

5. Ask them to join a partner and work together as a pair on the following short dialogues

Extract from *Dracula*

Van Helsing:	I come to destroy you, Count Dracula.
Dracula:	You cannot destroy me. I am stronger than you.
Van Helsing:	You fiend of hell!
Dracula:	Can you not feel my power?
Van Helsing:	I won't give in.
Dracula:	Already your eyes are closing.
Van Helsing:	I will not give in to your power.
Dracula:	You are feeling tired, drowsy and sleepy.
Van Helsing:	(weaker) I won't give in.

Dracula: Soon you will be completely asleep.
Van Helsing: Curse you, Dracula, curse you.
Dracula: Come to me now!
Van Helsing: No!
Dracula: Come to me now!

(Dracula draws Van Helsing to him with the power of his right hand. Van Helsing is powerless, his eyes go blank and he walks slowly towards Dracula.)

Dracula: Now, sit down and listen to what I say. You old fool!

6. The following dialogue can be done as pair work. The characters are a couple of pirates who taunt each other in an exaggerated, 'pirate-like' fashion. In contrast to the previous dialogue this should be played for comedy

Pirate 1: Aha! You dog!
Pirate 2: Aha! You scum!
Pirate 1: Do you think I'm gonna let you live now, you weasel!
Pirate 2: Do you think I'm gonna let *you* live now, you shrimp!
Pirate 1: (taking out cutlass) On guard, you piece of horseflesh!
Pirate 2: (taking out cutlass) On guard, you piece of lard!
Pirate 1: Have at you, you coward!
Pirate 2: Have at you, you jelly!

(They fight backwards and forwards. Appropriate music could be inserted for the sword-fight sequence.)

Pirate 1: (piercing him through) Gotcha! You vermin.

Pirate 2: (staggering) Aaaah! (recovering and stabbing him) Gotcha too, you big toad!

(They both fall over and die.)

Variations

- Items 5 and 6 could either be photocopied or copied out as part of an English lesson.

Walking

> The next two activities will explore the different ways in which certain types of characters move.

Suitable for

KS1, KS2

Cross-curriculum link

English

Aims

- To invent types of movement.
- To work as a team.

Resources

- An open space

What to do

1. As preparation for specific character movement ask the class to move around the room or studio in the following ways

    - walk with a purpose
    - walk aimlessly
    - walk as if you are late for an appointment
    - walk as if you are hurrying to get home for your tea
    - walk as if you are hurrying to get to the loo
    - walk hesitantly as if going to the dentist
    - walk slowly as if going to school
    - walk home as if it's your birthday.

2. Now ask the class to get into pairs. One of them is mum/dad and the other is a child. Repeat the following movement ideas
   - child walking aimlessly/mum hurrying her along
   - child walking to dentist/dad hurrying him along
   - child walking to school/mum hurrying him along
   - child late for an audition/mum hurrying her
   - child wants a specific item in a shop/dad tries to dissuade.

3. Now ask each pair to improvise some dialogue around each scene. Give them time to rehearse.

4. Each pair can then choose whichever scene they like best and perform it in front of the whole class.

Variations

- Try putting forward some further details for each scenario
  - you are walking to school in the snow
  - you are going to the dentist, it is raining
  - you are going home for tea and crossing a busy road.

Character Walks

> In this activity we focus on specific character types and the different ways they might move.

Suitable for

KS1, KS2

Cross-curriculum link

PE

Aims

- To observe movement.
- To work as a pair.
- To invent dialogue to suit character.

Resources

- An open space

What to do

1. Ask them to move as the following character types:

   - a soldier
   - a spy
   - a king
   - a queen
   - a prince

   - a princess
   - a security guard
   - a gangster
   - a policeman
   - a butler.

2. In pairs ask them to *mime* the following

   - two soldiers planning an attack
   - two spies meeting at dead of night
   - two gangsters planning a robbery.

3. Still in their pairs ask them to *mime* some action between the following pairs of characters

- a king and his cook
- a queen and her dressmaker
- a security guard and a famous person
- a policeman interviewing a criminal
- a butler and his master
- a maid and her mistress.

4. Ask them to add dialogue to the above scenes and perform some of them in front of the rest of the class.

Variations

- In item 2 above you could use the 'Mars' music from Holst's 'The Planets' to add atmosphere to the mimes.
- If any of the dialogues are particularly successful you could go to your props/costumes and develop the scene further with the use of crowns for the king and queen or a mob cap for servants, etc.

James Bond

In this session we use drama ideas to follow the activities of a modern cultural hero from the film world and to provide an opportunity for the children to explore their own heroes and heroines.

Suitable for

KS1, KS2

Cross-curriculum links

English, PE

Aims

- To improve your sense of timing.
- To list your heroes or heroines.

Resources

- An open space
- A sound recording of the main musical theme of the Bond films

What to do

1. Put on the James Bond music and ask the class to move in the following ways

   - move with your chest sticking out
   - move with your shoulders rolling
   - move with your hips swaying
   - move with head held high
   - turn and take out your gun
   - turn and shoot behind you
   - turn and shoot up above you

- turn and shoot ahead of you
- turn, take aim and fire into the far distance
- blow into your gun.

Turn the music off.

2. Ask the children to get into pairs. One of them is Bond, the other is the villain. Bond is having a game of cards with the villain. Try the following silent mime sequences in pairs

- both of you look at your cards
- both of you look at each other
- both of you look at your cards again
- the villain throws down a card on the table
- Bond picks it up and throws down another card
- the villain picks it up
- the villain smiles across at Bond
- Bond smiles back
- the villain puts down all his cards and smiles at Bond
- the villain goes to pick up all the money from the table
- Bond stops him
- Bond puts down all his cards
- the villain's smile disappears
- Bond smiles.

3. The above sequence can now be rehearsed, adding suitable dialogue and finding a suitable ending. Give the children some time to think about and rehearse their work. Go round and watch each group as they rehearse and make suitable suggestions for improvement. Ask groups to perform their pieces in front of the others if they wish to. Use the Bond music in the background if appropriate.

4. Give out a piece of blank paper to each child and make sure they have a pen or pencil. They need not put their name on the paper. Ask the class to think about any people they admire, either from a TV programme, the world of films or music, the world of sports, or any period of history. Ask them to write down a list of at least half a dozen people they most admire in order of preference. Make sure that they do not copy each other or talk during this activity. It is important that they write down what they think and not what somebody else thinks. Go round and help those who need assistance. After a while collect up the papers.

5. As a follow-up to what the children have just written, ask them all to stand in the middle of the room. Ask them to think about their first choice.

- Ask those who chose a famous singer or pop group to go to a corner of the room.
- Ask those who chose a sporting personality to go to another corner of the room.
- Ask those who chose a famous actor, TV star or film star to go to another corner of the room.
- Ask those who chose a famous character from history to go to the final corner of the room.
- Any one left is to remain in the middle of the room.

Now ask all the groups to show you their characters, all at the same time as follows

- as a freeze-frame photograph
- doing what they are famous for as a mime without words.

Now ask the whole class to sit down. Each person who wants to can demonstrate who they are and the class has to guess who they are.

Variations

- You can have three guessing sessions
    - mime only
    - with sound
    - with speech.

Animal Movement (The Cat)

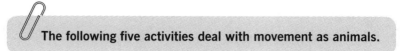

The following five activities deal with movement as animals.

Suitable for

KS1, KS2

Cross-curriculum link

PE

Aims

- To be flexible in the joints of the body.
- To realise the importance of facial expression.
- To control different parts of the body.

Resources

- An open space

What to do

1. In order to energise the body ask the children to spread out and do the following exercises

   - hands high above head
   - stretch up as far as you can
   - extend arms sideways
   - stretch out as far as you can
   - hands by your side and stiffen the arms
   - now relax the arms
   - now stiffen the arms
   - now relax and stiffen the arms six times
   - now bend the elbows six times
   - bend the wrists
   - now bend the elbows and the wrists alternately.

2. Now concentrate on the legs, knees and feet

- stand on tiptoe and down again
- repeat ten times
- bend the knees
- repeat ten times
- now jump as high as you can
- repeat six times
- now stand on toes, bend the knees and jump as high as you can.

3. Ask them to lie on the floor comfortably then slowly start to stand in the smoothest manner possible until they are fully standing. Slowly stretch out their arms as far as they can. Then do everything in reverse until they are lying on the floor again in the same position they started out.

4. Now ask them to use their hands, wrists and arms to create a cat's paws

- cleaning behind its ears
- scratching a tree to sharpen its claws
- attacking a mouse.

5. Now as a cat jump up on to a chair

- start washing yourself
- jump down and eat your food
- curl up and go to sleep.

6. Now we'll concentrate on the cat's facial expression

- the cat is smiling
- the cat is expecting its food
- the cat sees its owner
- the owner walks past
- the cat does not get any food
- the cat is sad
- the cat becomes angry
- the owner comes back
- the owner has remembered
- the owner opens a tin of cat food
- the cat is expectant
- the cat gets its food
- the cat is happy
- the cat curls up and goes to sleep.

7. Ask the class to make the following movements as the cat

- the cat asleep
- the cat waking up
- the cat stretching
- the cat walking
- the cat going through a cat flap
- the cat sniffing in the garden.

8. Now ask the class to make the following cat movements as slowly as possible

- waking up from a deep sleep
- cleaning behind the ears
- hearing a strange sound
- moving five paces
- arching its back
- realising it's an enemy cat
- getting ready to spring.

Variations

- The slow-motion sections can be played as 'games', with the *last* person to finish being the winner.
- You could ask them to pair up and do some of the movements together.
- Music is very helpful for some of these exercises – suggestions are in the Appendix.

Animal Movement (Fish)

In this activity children are asked to imitate the actions of fish.

Suitable for

KS1, KS2

Cross-curriculum link

PE

Aims

- To coordinate movement.
- To watch others.
- To listen carefully.
- To sharpen one's sense of rhythm.

Resources

- An open space
- CD music of 'Carnival of the Animals'

What to do

1. Before starting the fish movements do some initial physical exercises to help them to move smoothly
   - waggle your fingers quickly
   - waggle your fingers slowly
   - waggle your hands from the wrists
   - move your arms slowly from the elbows downwards
   - move your arms slowly from the shoulders
   - make both arms do the same slow movement
   - bend at the elbows smoothly and slowly

- move both arms up and down together
- move both arms backwards and forwards together
- imagine you are a fish swimming
- your arms are fins
- your arms make your body swim fast
- your arms make your body swim slowly
- puff out your cheeks
- put the palms of your hands together
- move as smoothly as you can as a fish.

2. Ask the children to imagine that the room is a vast aquarium filled with water and that they are all fish swimming around. Ask them to stay on their feet and use their arms as fins to propel themselves forward.

3. After they have all had a practice together ask them to swim to the side of the aquarium and have a rest. Each person in the class should now be asked to swim round the aquarium one at a time, using whatever fish movement they like. You can suggest the following ideas to them

- a very small fish
- a very big fish
- a skinny fish
- a fat fish
- a flat fish
- a beautiful fish
- an ugly fish
- an exotic fish.

4. Now everyone can join in again, but this time suggest the following characteristics, which will change the movement

- a shy fish who is scared
- a snooty fish who is very proud
- a young fish who is lost
- a naughty fish
- a sleepy fish
- an energetic fish
- a sad fish.

5. Next have a round in which you can suggest that each person creates a fish that is in complete contrast to the person who went before them.

6. Now ask them to pair up with someone and swim together, doing the same rhythmic movement. Put on some music after they have had a practice and let each pair have a go on their own, swimming twice around the space.

7. Then ask them to join another pair to make up a group of four. Put on the same music as they are swimming and ask them to really concentrate so that they are all swimming in formation. You could suggest the following ideas

- swim side by side in a line
- swim one behind the other
- swim very spread out
- swim in a tight bunch.

8. If you feel the class can do it, ask them to make a group of eight or use the whole class together swimming in formation to the music.

Variations

- Initial exercises for the upper part of the body could be practised by
  - sitting cross-legged on the floor
  - kneeling
  - lying on their backs.
- When they start to move you ask them to move
  - on tiptoe
  - bending the knees
  - moving on flat feet.

Animal Movement (The Tortoise)

 This session continues the imitation of the movement of certain animals.

Suitable for

KS1, KS2

Cross-curriculum link

PE

Aims

- To move together.
- To practise facial movement.
- To observe.
- To keep in rhythm.

Resources

- An open space
- A CD of the tortoise music from 'Carnival of the Animals'
- Woolly hats (optional)

What to do

1. Ask the class for words or phrases that come to mind when they think of a tortoise.

2. Use the following initial exercises on the shape of the body in preparation for tortoise movements

   - put the palms of your hands and your knees firmly on the floor
   - show me the palms of your hands
   - imagine your hands are twice as big and heavy
   - place your palms on the floor

- show me your hands again
- imagine your hands are three times larger and very heavy
- place your hands on the floor again
- slowly lift one heavy hand from the floor
- slowly put it back again
- slowly lift the other heavy hand
- slowly put it back again
- arch your back
- move your face without touching it
- make an old face
- very slowly start to move forward as the tortoise.

3. Ask them to find a partner and kneel opposite them with their faces almost touching. Ask them to move various parts of the face to make their partner laugh

- move the nose
- move the lips
- show your teeth
- stare with your eyes
- half close your eyes
- move your eyebrows up and down
- smile
- move your nose to one side
- move your nose to the other side
- move your lips to one side
- move your lips to the other side
- press your lips together hard
- keep your face still and look right
- keep your face still and look left
- look at your partner
- look up and then look down
- make an ugly face
- make a beautiful face
- make the ugliest face you can
- make a young face
- make an old face
- make a really old face
- make a tortoise face.

4. Tell them that they will have to work with their partner to create the impression of two tortoises moving together at exactly the same slow speed round the room. They will also be doing facial expressions as well. In order to help them put on the tortoise music.

5. Ask the pairs to lie on their backs side by side and then ask them to do the following movements

- lift their legs up off the ground
- bring their knees up to their waist
- raise their arms
- in this position gently sway from side to side
- after six sways turn over on to their knees and palms
- repeat the process with their partner
- start from the beginning until they both turn over at the same time.

6. Ask the pairs to start from sitting on their knees and palms and then proceed to walk together as two tortoises side by side.

7. They could now pair up and make a group of four tortoises. Repeat the same movements with each group attempting to move together in time to the music.

8. Suggest a family of tortoises going for a walk together

- father tortoise
- mother tortoise
- two young tortoises.

Variations

- The music CD can be used at all stages of the development of these movements.
- Each round of movement could be a game in which the most coordinated children win an award of a woolly hat.
- You could vary the movements of the tortoises by calling out
  - left turn
  - right turn
  - reverse
  - straight ahead
  - move in a circle
  - walk in a figure eight.

Animal Movement (Birds and Insects)

We learn in this activity how to give the impression through movement of various kinds of bird and insect.

Suitable for

KS1, KS2

Cross-curriculum link

PE

Aims

- To focus on working together.
- To concentrate on timing.
- To gain physical control.

Resources

- An open space
- CD of 'Carnival of the Animals'
- Some chairs

What to do

1. In order to get into the mood of bird movement the following exercises could be suggested, with all the class standing separately

   - flap hands and wrists quickly
   - flap hands and wrists slowly
   - flap whole arms up and down slowly, bending the elbows
   - flap whole arms up and down slowly, not bending the elbows
   - stand on toes and bend knees, going up and down slowly
   - stand quite still and suddenly look left and then right
   - stand quite still and suddenly look up and down
   - repeat all the above exercises.

2. After these exercises ask the children what size of bird each movement suggests and ask them to name the birds if possible.

3. Now ask them to imitate with their arms and movement the following birds

   - seagulls
   - robins
   - crows
   - sparrows
   - eagles
   - pigeons.

4. Using the music stimuli for the various birds ask the children to get into pairs or groups. Each group must give the impression of birds in flight but keeping together so that they fly in formation. The following variations could be suggested

   - gliding
   - swooping
   - turning
   - perching
   - landing.

5. Now concentrate on the swan. Put on the music for the swan and let them hear it first without doing any movement. You can suggest the following key words to them

   - elegance
   - smoothness
   - neck held high.

6. Put them or let them arrange themselves into groups for the movement session of 'the swan'. Groups should be no larger than five. They must keep together as with all other previous bird movements and you could suggest the following scenario

   - group of swans gliding in the water
   - they take off and fly
   - they gently land on the water again.

7. This activity is called 'the bee' and demands a totally different style of movement. Ask them to get into pairs or groups as before and suggest the following scenarios to follow

   - bees hovering
   - bees smell flowers
   - they land on the flowers
   - they nuzzle the blossom
   - they fly away as a human approaches.

8. The following movement of wasps can be done with the children making their own sound effects, so no music is necessary here. Ask each group to work together to convey the following story with sound effects provided by them

- group of wasps hovering around a pot of jam
- they land on the jam making appropriate sounds
- they eat greedily
- they fly off as a human swats them.

Variations

- The seagull movements in item 3 would be enhanced by the children making the appropriate sounds.
- With the bee scenario in item 7 the story could include a human who is working in the garden.
- With the wasp scenario in item 8 the story could include a human who is stung by the wasps.
- The children should be encouraged to create their own scenarios (without speech) for any of the bird types mentioned.

Animal Movement (Kangaroos and Cuckoos)

This activity deals with movement ideas based on the music of Saint-Saën's 'Carnival of the Animals'.

Suitable for

KS1, KS2

Cross-curriculum link

PE

Aims

- To listen carefully.
- To learn precise movement.
- To work as a team.

Resources

- A CD of 'Carnival of the Animals'

What to do

1. Ask the class to spread out. Make sure they have plenty of individual space. Ask them to swing their arms to make sure they are not touching anyone then give them the following activities

   - spring up as high as you can
   - bounce up and down on the spot ten times
   - bounce up and down like a big kangaroo
   - bounce up and down like a baby kangaroo
   - bounce up and down like a giant kangaroo.

2. Now continue with the following movement ideas

- bounce forward like a kangaroo three times then stop still
- turn your head to right and left
- turn your head to right and left and sniff the air
- bounce forward twice then stand still
- sniff the air
- turn your head right and left as if you sense danger
- now repeat the bouncing, the standing still, the head turning and the sense of danger.

3. Put on the music track for 'kangaroos' from the 'Carnival of the Animals' and ask the class to do the same movements as above. They should bounce when the music goes fast and stand still, looking right and left, when the music goes slow.

4. Get the class into kangaroo family groups of four or five with two adults and two or three baby kangaroos. Ask the groups to rehearse to the music trying to communicate a sense of danger. When they have rehearsed for five minutes ask each group to perform in front of the rest of the class.

5. Now ask them to remain in their groups but this time they are going to be cuckoos. Ask them to stand in a circle and listen to the cuckoo music from 'Carnival of the Animals'. When they hear the 'cuckoo sound' they must all bow forward. The groups will have to concentrate on listening carefully because the cuckoo sounds come at irregular intervals. It is great fun waiting for the cuckoo sounds. The whole family must bow at the same time.

6. Ask each group to stand on chairs in a circle and perform in front of the rest of the class to see which cuckoo group can bow at the same time best. No talking allowed.

7. Ask the groups to imagine they are in a cuckoo clock and must come out and say 'cuckoo' on the hour. Each group can rehearse their own special movement as they step out. They must all step out and 'cuckoo' at the same time. When they have rehearsed their movement and their timing you can 'test' each group by calling out a time (e.g. three o'clock, six o'clock, etc.) and the groups must work in harmony to produce precise group movement and precise cuckoo chimes. The winner is the group with the best sense of timing.

Looking and Listening

> In this activity we learn how important it is to observe people and objects around us and to listen carefully to sounds in the real world.

Suitable for

KS1, KS2

Cross-curriculum link

Music

Aims

- To observe.
- To remember what has been seen.
- To describe what has been seen.
- To listen carefully.
- To follow the rhythms of others.

Resources

- CD of aerobic music. See Appendix for details.

What to do

1. Get the children to stand in a circle and put on some slow, hypnotic music. (There are various suggestions in the Appendix.) Ask them to keep their feet still but they can move any other part of the body in any way they like, following the rhythm of the music in their own personal manner.

2. Ask for a volunteer to be 'the centre of attention'. This person moves – feet completely still remember – in any way they choose and the rest of the circle have to follow their movements as close as possible. The

music will be slow, so it will be relatively easy for the class to follow the movement. After a while (say 30 seconds) this first person points to someone else in the circle who becomes the focus of attention and everyone follows *their* movements, and so on until everyone has had a go at being the centre of attention. They are only allowed one turn each as centre of attention so children have to remember who has gone before so they don't pick them again. No talking allowed. Everyone is watching, concentrating and following movements.

3. Put on some fast aerobic dance music – again there are various suggestions in the Appendix – and do the same as above.

4. Ask the class to sit down on the floor or on chairs if more appropriate. They must now look at and remember as many objects in the room as possible. Give them ten seconds, then they must close their eyes. Ask different people to list as many objects as they can.

5. Now tell them that they must choose an object in the room and describe it in as much detail as possible – shape, colour, texture. Give them ten seconds then they must close their eyes. Ask different people to describe their chosen object. They must all have their eyes closed while describing the objects.

6. Next ask the class to look at the positions of everyone around the room and then after ten seconds to close their eyes. Pick people to point to where everyone is sitting, saying their names as they point. The person who is 'it' has ten seconds to look and then he/she closes their eyes. The rest of the class, of course, can have their eyes open. The winner is the person who can name the most people and where they are sitting correctly.

7. Ask the class to sit in a circle, close their eyes and listen to sounds coming from

- as far away as possible
- outside the room
- inside the room.

After about 30 seconds ask them to open their eyes and tell you what they heard for the three distances. Repeat the exercise to see if anything else can be added to the list of things heard.

8. Still sitting in the circle, ask them to close their eyes and then you tap someone on the shoulder. That person can open their eyes and must move as quietly as possible around the room. The rest of the class have to listen carefully and point to wherever that person goes in the room. Complete silence is essential for this.

Variations

- In items 2 and 3 the teacher could specify that only certain parts of the body must move to the music and therefore the class only follow the movement of, for example, arms, hands, head and shoulders, waist, feet, one foot!
- In item 5 (where the children are asked to describe an object verbally) you could ask them to draw the object or write the description on paper or in their English book.
- For item 6 you could ask the class to all change places and the person who is 'it' has ten seconds to remember where everyone is sitting before he/she closes their eyes.

Making Statues

In this activity children work in pairs to make recognisable 'statues' out of their partners and then add movement to them.

Suitable for

KS1, KS2

Cross-curriculum link

PE

Aims

- To learn the importance of posture.
- To learn the discipline of being still.
- To work with others.
- To speak as a character.

Resources

- An open space

What to do

1. Ask the class to think of a statue, any statue that they have ever seen. Then ask them to walk around the room thinking of their statue shape. When you clap your hands they must freeze in the position of their chosen statue. Do this a number of times until the children get used to moving and freezing.

2. You can inspect each statue and guess what it is.

3. Ask them to get into pairs. One of them is A, the other is B
   - A and B are made of plasticine and walk in a very floppy manner
   - A and B are made of stone and walk very stiffly
   - A is made of plasticine and B is made of stone. They walk in their appropriate manner
   - A is made of stone and B is made of plasticine. They walk in their appropriate manner.

4. Now they will work together to create a sculpture figure

- A is the sculptor and B is a formless figure made of soft plasticine
- B is nothing and waits for A to make a shape out of him/her
- A makes B into a 'teacher' sculpture
- B makes A into a 'king' sculpture
- A makes B into a dog
- B makes A into a monkey
- A makes B into a soldier
- B makes A into a witch
- A makes B into a teapot
- B makes A into a vase of flowers.

5. Ask the class to spread out as individuals. They will now form the sculpture shapes they created previously. You call out the name of the sculpture and each member of the class will freeze into the shape

- teacher
- king
- dog
- monkey
- soldier
- witch
- teapot
- vase of flowers.

6. This time call out a sculpture shape randomly in any order and the class will

- freeze in the correct shape
- come to life and speak when you say so.

7. You could try the following 'statues' freezing and coming to life

- tennis player
- netball player
- footballer
- cricketer
- darts player
- snooker player
- boxer.

8. Now choose one person to be a sculpture. The rest of the class must join in and become characters associated with the main sculpture. For example, if you call out 'priestess', the rest of the class can be worshippers bowing down to her. They all come to life and speak or chant when you say so. Try the following and pick a new person each time to be the main character

- priestess
- orchestra conductor
- cameraman
- airline pilot
- supermarket manager
- lion tamer
- the Queen.

All Aboard!

In this activity we do individual and group movement associated with boats and ships. Suitable music is suggested in the Appendix.

Suitable for

KS1 (optional), KS2

Cross-curriculum links

PE, Music

Aims

- To work as a large group.
- To listen to instructions.
- To practise self-discipline.

Resources

- An open space
- Sailors' hats or white T-shirts
- CD of 'Scheherazade' music (see Appendix)

What to do

1. Ask the class to form the shape of a boat. Put one person at the bow (front) and one person at the stern (back). The rest of the class arrange themselves so that they're all facing in the same direction (i.e. towards the front of the boat). Feet firmly planted on the floor. If the person at the bow leans to the left all the class lean to the left. If the person leans to the right they all lean to the right. Practise with the whole class. They must not move their feet. A gentle rocking motion is all that is required here. Practise until everyone is moving together. Gentle music from 'Scheherazade' would enhance the effect.

2. Explain that starboard means 'right' and port means 'left' on a boat. When the teacher calls out 'port' all the class move to the left of the boat. When the teacher calls 'starboard' all the class move to the right. No falling over at this stage. No one falls overboard – yet. It is still a relatively calm sea.

3. Ask them to find a partner and stick to that partner whichever direction the boat moves. Call out 'port' and 'starboard' again.

4. Ask them now to listen for 'bow' and 'stern'. When you call out 'bow' the class move towards the front of the boat. When you call out 'stern' the class move to the back of the boat. They should stay in their pairs.

5. Now call out any of the instructions – 'port', 'starboard', 'bow' or 'stern' – in random order. The class must all move in the correct direction. Suitable music will create the right atmosphere, such as 'Scheherazade'.

6. Next add the instruction 'up' and 'down'. When you call 'down' the class will all bend their knees. When you call 'up' the class will stand up straight again.

7. Now call out a random selection of the six instructions. The class must go in the direction indicated.

Variations

- The person at the bow of the boat could stand on a chair to be seen by everyone and point left and right. The class follow the direction indicated. Music can be used here.
- Different pupils can volunteer to be the 'bow' person.
- You could give everyone in the class a number. When you call out their number he/she becomes the 'bow' person.

Jobs (part 1)

For this activity prepare a series of cards with the names of professions or jobs written clearly on each card.

Suitable for

KS1, KS2

Cross-curriculum link

English

Aims

- To work as a pair.
- To work as a group.

Resources

- An open space
- A set of cards with the names of jobs written on them

What to do

1. Tell the children that you have a set of cards with the names of jobs that people do. When you call out a job the children must mime the activity on their own without involving anyone else in the class. Call out the following

   - a tailor
   - a cook
   - a watchmaker
   - a plumber
   - a gardener
   - a scientist

- a sculptor
- a priest
- a secretary
- a cleaner.

2. Ask the children to choose a partner and without talking to mime the following jobs together

   - a barber
   - a hairdresser
   - a cricket player
   - a netball player
   - a teacher
   - a dentist
   - a lion tamer
   - a butler
   - a fortune teller
   - a waiter.

3. Now ask the children to repeat the last ten jobs and create a scene with words involving two characters. Give them time to rehearse and go round to see what they are doing. Towards the end of the session you can let the children choose any of the scenes they have done to perform in front of the class.

4. Now ask the children to get into groups of four. Call out one job from your cards and ask the children to create a mime involving all four of them together. There must be no talking or discussion. They must start as soon as they can

   - a fireman
   - a shelf-stacker in a supermarket
   - an onion seller
   - a barman
   - a window cleaner.

5. Now ask each group of four to create an improvisation based around any of the previous five jobs. Give them time to rehearse and go round the class to see how they are getting on. At the end of the session they can perform their scenes in front of the class.

Variations

- The groups could be asked to think up their own jobs or professions and create a scene around them.

Jobs (part 2)

This session contains more jobs and professions around which the children can create mimes or improvisations.

Suitable for

KS1, KS2

Cross-curriculum links

English, PE

Aims

- To work by oneself.
- To work with a partner.
- To work in a group.

Resources

- An open space
- Job cards

What to do

1. In this first task ask the pupils to pick or point to one of the cards you are holding, read it and then proceed to mime what is on the card. Younger children sometimes like to close their eyes and select a card. This ensures that there can be no cheating. The children should not be allowed to pick another card if they don't like the one they've selected. It is more challenging to do the one they've picked first, even though they may not like it. The rest of the class watch and have to guess what the job is. Ask the class not to call out until the mime is finished.

2. Ask the children to choose a partner. One of the pair chooses a card from the teacher, then the pair takes it away and starts to rehearse a

mime. Give out as many cards as necessary for the children all to get on and rehearse their mimes. After a few minutes call time and invite each pair to show the rest of the class their job mime.

3. The children can now add speech to their mime and create a scene.

4. Now the whole class can work together on the following activity. Call out a job and point to someone in the class. That person must teach the rest of the class how to do that job. Here are some suggestions

- how to boil an egg
- how to make a bed
- how to be a good waiter or waitress
- how to mop a floor
- how to clean windows
- how to cut someone's hair
- how to tidy a bedroom
- how to be nice to customers in a shop.

5. In groups of four ask pupils to create a TV advert for the following

- girl's eyeliner
- washing powder
- babies' nappies
- shampoo for humans
- shampoo for dogs
- cupcakes.

Jobs (part 3)

In this final session on jobs we look at more ways of using drama to help us identify people who work in more unusual professions.

Suitable for

KS1, KS2

Cross-curriculum link

English

Aims

- To work as a group.
- To listen and follow others.
- To use their imagination.

Resources

- An open space

What to do

1. Ask the class to spread out and stand by themselves. Tell them you are going to introduce them to jobs that are unusual. They should use any mime they think suitable to express the movement involved in these activities

   - bell ringer
   - mask maker
   - mountaineer
   - kung-fu learner
   - skier
   - tightrope walker

- astronomer
- opera singer
- magician
- monk
- glassblower
- goldsmith.

2. Now ask them to find a partner and together work on devising a mime which reflects the job.

3. After they have rehearsed each mime have a performance session in which each pair acts out their favourite activity in front of the class.

4. Now you can introduce speech into the activity. Ask for one partner in each pair to teach one of the skills to their partner.

5. Finally ask the class to follow one person who will be the focal point of an activity. Point to one person in the class and tell them that they will have to play the role of, for example, a priestess. The rest of the class have to do whatever the priestess does or says. Once they have got used to the idea of making that person the focal point, they should all look at that one person and obey them. You can try the following jobs or professions in the same way

- a conductor of an orchestra
- a photographer
- a teacher
- a king
- a traffic warden
- Her Majesty the Queen
- the Prime Minister
- any famous singer
- any famous actor or actress
- God.

Expressive Mime (The Letter)

In this and the next three activities we focus on the power of expressive mime and telling a story without words.

Suitable for

KS1, KS2

Cross-curriculum links

English, PE

Aims

- To demonstrate coordination.
- To show imitation.
- To learn the importance of adjectives.

Resources

- Pen, paper and envelopes

What to do

1. Ask the class to spread out and express mainly with their feet and legs the following actions

   - skipping
   - being a kangaroo
   - being a frog in a marsh
   - walking like a tortoise
   - walking like a cat
   - being a jack-in-the-box in action.

2. Now movements largely for the head but the rest of the body can join in as well

   - show the neck and head of a giraffe
   - show an ostrich looking around and then hiding its head in the sand
   - be a puppet on a string

- show a bird pecking for crumbs
- show a very proud person
- show a reaction to a very bad smell.

3. Now for some very flexible movements using the torso

- be a rubber toy, flabby at first
- now someone blows air into them
- they are nearly bursting
- then the bung is removed and they collapse.

4. They should try the last exercise with a partner

- who blows them up with a pump
- puts a cork in them
- then removes the cork.

Reverse the roles. They can make any sound they like when the cork is removed.

5. Then they can try the following with their partner

- being a couple of worms
- being a couple of seals
- playing with a ball
- being a couple of butterflies.

6. Now they should face each other and show the following facial reactions

- surprise
- fear
- horror.

7. Now ask them to try the following with their partner

- they are given a letter
- they open the letter
- they read the letter
- they are told in the letter that they have won a competition
- they give a letter to their partner
- they open the letter
- they read the letter
- they are told in the letter that they have failed their exams.

8. Now ask the pairs to write a real letter to each other in which one of them has won a competition and the other has failed their exams. The letter must be sealed then each pair takes a turn at opening the letter and reacting appropriately. The rest of the class can watch.

Expressive Mime (The Window Cleaners)

> We continue learning about how expressive the body can be in communicating meaning to an audience.

Suitable for

KS1, KS2

Cross-curriculum link

PE

Aims

- To work in harmony with others.
- To listen to instructions.
- To use the imagination.

Resources

- Plastic bucket and an old cloth

What to do

1. Ask them to find a partner and express the following ideas in mime only, as if in

   - a very strong wind
   - a hailstorm
   - a snowstorm
   - a thunderstorm
   - rain
   - a sandstorm
   - a gale.

2. Still with their partner ask them to show the differences in their feelings as they walk

   - on a mountain track
   - on quicksand
   - on desert sand
   - on rock
   - through jungle.

3. Still working together with their partner they now imagine they are travelling

- on a horse
- on skis
- in a car
- on a bicycle
- on a mule
- on a sledge.
- in a boat

4. Now they join with another pair to make up a group of four (five is acceptable but six is too many). Show through expressive mime by working with their group that they are in

- a tent
- an igloo
- a palace
- a castle
- a mud hut
- a museum.

5. In their groups of four show that they are

- fishing
- doing basket work
- sheep shearing
- doing factory work
- working in the kitchen of a busy restaurant.

6. In their groups they are now going to tell the following story in mime. The story is called 'The Window Cleaners'

- a rich home owner telephones a firm of window cleaners to come and clean the windows of his house
- three window cleaners arrive in their van
- they knock on the door and the owner shows them what is to be done
- they set up their ladders
- the owner goes into his library to read *The Times* and have a cup of tea
- the window cleaners climb up and down ladders cleaning windows
- one of the window cleaners crashes a ladder accidentally through a window
- fortunately the owner has fallen asleep and does not hear the crash
- one of the window cleaners goes off to buy a new pane of glass
- the other two window cleaners continue cleaning
- the owner stirs in his chair but does not wake up
- the other window cleaner arrives with a new pane of glass
- as he takes it out of the van he drops it and it smashes

- the other two window cleaners hit him with their caps
- the window cleaners clear up the mess quickly
- the owner wakes up and comes outside
- the owner looks up at the house and notices the broken window
- the window cleaners beg him not to report them
- they blame it on the clumsiness of their stupid colleague
- the owner refuses to pay them until they've replaced the broken pane of glass.

Expressive Mime (The Tramp)

In this activity there is another opportunity for children to express themselves through individual and group mime.

Suitable for

KS1, KS2

Cross-curriculum link

PE

Aims

- To work in harmony with others.
- To show physical expressiveness.

Resources

- Props such as an umbrella, a briefcase, an old coat, a scarf, a policeman's helmet, etc.

What to do

1. Ask the class to spread out and find a space for themselves where they are going to do some individual mime work. Hands are very expressive. Ask the class to put out their hands and look at them. They should imagine their hands are going to be photographed and there will be a caption under each photograph. The first caption says

   - strong hands.

   Show me a photograph of strong hands.

   Now try the following

   - gentle hands
   - fierce hands
   - flabby hands
   - magic hands
   - nervous hands
   - begging hands.

2. Ask them to find a partner and go through the same process again. This time they have to express a photograph involving both of them. Same captions as above.

3. The next step is to tell them that they must now create a photograph in which they each have different types of hands. Ask them to create a photograph expressing the following

   - one of you has frozen hands, the other has warm hands
   - one of you has fierce hands, the other has gentle hands
   - one of you has hands that say 'stop', the other has hands that say 'silence'
   - one of you has hands that say 'keep away', the other has hands that say 'I love you'
   - one of you has healthy hands, the other has weak hands
   - one of you has old hands, the other has young hands.

4. Ask them to join another group making up groups of four. This time the whole group must create a still photograph expressing the following with their hands and facial expressions

   - greedy hands
   - kind hands
   - cruel hands
   - frightened hands.

5. Ask them now to decide who is going to play the following parts in the forthcoming scene

   - a posh person
   - a fat person
   - a policeman
   - a tramp.

6. When they have decided who is going to be who ask them to practise the following

   - walking as their character
   - showing the hands of the character
   - eating and drinking as the character
   - getting dressed in the morning as their character
   - doing their job as the character.

7. Now ask them to work on the following mime scenario
   - a posh businessman sits on a park bench
   - it is lunchtime and a policeman is patrolling the park
   - a fat man sits on the park bench and starts eating his lunch
   - the posh man expresses disgust at what he is eating
   - a tramp enters and starts to pick up the fat man's leftovers
   - the posh man goes up to the policeman and complains
   - the policeman orders the tramp off
   - the posh man sits on another bench and takes out his sandwiches
   - the tramp sits beside him
   - the posh man moves away
   - the fat man continues eating
   - the tramp sits between them
   - the fat man and the posh man get up and sit on another bench
   - the tramp sits between them again
   - they both go and complain to the policeman.

8. Ask the groups to end the scene in any way they like. Using props and some costumes would help the expressive nature of the scene, as would some background music.

Variations

- If the pupils wish to add dialogue to the scenario they could do so, but only after having rehearsed the storyline in mime.

Expressive Mime (The Report and The Cake)

In this activity we continue to work on ways of expressing meaning through the use of mime, ending up with another scenario for the children to act out.

Suitable for

KS1, KS2

Cross-curriculum link

PE

Aims

- To work closely with others.
- To observe.
- To listen carefully.

Resources

- Pieces of printed paper

What to do

1. Ask them to get into pairs and express the following mimes
   - sitting reading quietly, and there is a sudden clap of thunder
   - walking arm in arm and one of you trips
   - going into the sea on a cold day
   - pulling a cracker together
   - listening to the radio, one smells burning, the other remembers there is a cake in the oven
   - in a street, one is on a ladder cleaning windows, the other walking underneath, a wet cloth drops on his/her head
   - in a restaurant, one is a waiter who spills soup down the customer's neck.

2. They continue working in the same pairs or change partners if they wish

   - a pupil brings in a late piece of homework for a teacher
   - in a classroom a teacher is marking work quietly, a pupil barges in and falls over, the teacher gives her a punishment
   - in the head's study, the head is marking work, a pupil knocks and enters, the head shows the pupil his report, which is excellent
   - at home, the pupil shows his good report to mum
   - at home, a pupil shows her terrible report to mum.

3. Ask the children to try to express the following reactions through their mime. Ask them to stand as far away from each other as possible and then walk towards each other until they meet

   - the meeting is unexpected
   - the meeting is pleasant
   - the meeting is unpleasant
   - the meeting is awkward
   - the meeting is frightening
   - the meeting is embarrassing.

4. Ask them now to get into groups of four and consider the following characters for a scenario called 'The School Report'

   - clever pupil
   - dim pupil
   - mum
   - dad.

5. This is the scenario they should rehearse in their groups

   - the family is eating breakfast
   - they hear the post arriving
   - they all know it is the day on which reports arrive
   - mum goes to collect the post
   - she comes in and opens the good report
   - the good pupil beams and smiles
   - dad opens the bad report
   - it is terrible
   - the dim pupil bursts into tears.

   End it any way you like.

6. Ask the pupils to invent a different storyline about a report and add dialogue to it.

7. Tell them that the next scenario is based on someone sitting on a cream cake at a children's party. The characters are as follows

- posh mum who is giving the party for her daughter's birthday
- posh daughter
- posh friends
- a shy girl from across the road.

8. The suggested scenario for 'The Cake' is as follows

- posh friends arriving at posh house
- greeted by posh mum and daughter
- they each have a present for her
- she is spoilt rotten
- mum gives her a pretty new dress
- she goes off and puts it on
- she comes back and everyone admires her dress
- they start to have their tea
- the shy girl arrives late
- they all look down on her because she is not rich
- they all talk together and ignore her
- mum gives the shy girl a big cream cake
- she sits on her own and eats the cake
- the other girls dance and play together
- mum asks the shy girl to join the others
- the shy girl puts her half-eaten cream cake on the seat beside her and joins the others
- they all dance together
- the posh daughter gets tired and goes and sits down
- right on the cream cake in her new dress!

Ask the groups to either end it there or continue with their own invented ending.

Monsieur Hulot

Monsieur Hulot was a character created and played by French comedy actor, Jacques Tati, for a series of films in the 1950s. He is recognised by his overcoat, pipe and hat and his distinctive walk. If you are able to show the children the DVD of *Monsieur Hulot's Holiday*, they will learn a lot about movement and how it can be used in drama to communicate ideas as well as comedy.

Suitable for

KS1, KS2

Cross-curriculum links

English, History, PE, Modern Languages

Aims

- To use facial expression.
- To use bodily posture.

Resources

- A pipe
- A suitcase
- A crank handle
- A copy of the DVD *Monsieur Hulot's Holiday*.

What to do

1. Ask the children to try the following
   - walk with an imaginary pipe in your mouth
   - walk with an imaginary pipe in your mouth and your arms behind your back

- lean forward as you walk
- now look up and see something in the distance
- take the pipe out of your mouth
- you see a young lady who is struggling with a heavy suitcase.

Try the whole sequence again and memorise it as a piece of mime that tells a story.

2. In pairs, one partner is Hulot, the other is the young lady. Without speaking they should try to convey the following ideas

- greet the young lady
- indicate that you wish to help her with her suitcase
- she does not understand
- explain again
- now she understands
- she indicates some steps
- you pick up her suitcase
- it is heavier than you thought
- you struggle with it up the steps
- she tries to help
- you refuse her help
- you struggle with the suitcase
- you fall over
- she helps you up
- you try again to go up the steps
- with great effort you get to the top
- you look pleased with yourself
- then you lose your balance and fall over.

Each group can rehearse the whole sequence as a silent mime and perform it in front of the class. As an addition they can use a real suitcase.

3. In groups of three rehearse the following sequence of mime in which a car breaks down and Hulot tries to crank it up to start.

One person is Hulot, the other two are passengers

- the car stops with a judder and a lot of noise
- Hulot presses the ignition
- the car judders again and refuses to start
- Hulot tries the ignition once again

- the car judders and stops
- Hulot gets out of the car
- he gets the crank handle from the boot
- he goes round to the front of the car
- he inserts the crank handle at the front
- he turns it suddenly
- it does not start
- he tries again
- it does not start
- one of the passengers tries
- the car refuses to start
- the third passenger, who is the smallest and youngest, gets out
- he offers to help
- the other two refuse
- they laugh at him
- he grabs the crank handle, inserts it and turns
- the car starts immediately
- they all pile in and drive off.

4. Hulot, as you can see from the film, is accident prone. He is a very nice man but almost always causes chaos. Choose any comedy sequence from the film and work in groups of four or five to recreate it in mime.

Variations

Once the children have seen the film they can choose any sequence involving mime and create the scene in groups

- the sequence at the railway station
- the tennis match
- Hulot in the canoe
- the dining room sequence.

Gesture

This activity deals with communicating meaning through hand gestures.

Suitable for

KS1, KS2

Cross-curriculum link

English

Aims

- To express meaning with hands.
- To express meaning with facial expression.

Resources

- An open space

What to do

1. Explain that they are now going to speak with their hands. It is called the art of gesture. Start by asking them to use their hands

   - as if they were washing with soap and water
   - as if the water was very cold
   - as if the water was very hot
   - as if the weather was very cold
   - as if the weather was very hot
   - as if they were thinking about money
   - as if they were thinking about a lot of money
   - as if they were counting stolen money
   - as if they'd done something really wicked
   - as if they were very hungry
   - as if they were looking forward to a good meal.

2. Now ask them to repeat the above gestures adding strong facial expressions.

3. Ask them to use their hands and faces to express the following

- being really bored
- waiting for the bus
- thinking really hard about a maths problem
- dreaming about a holiday in the sun
- realising they haven't done their homework
- realising they've lost their house keys
- realising they've lost their money
- having to tell their parents they've failed their maths test.

4. Now ask them to focus on their index finger to express the following

- wagging their finger to tell someone off
- accusing someone of stealing their sandwiches
- pointing to the head's study
- pointing the way along the road
- pointing up a hill
- pointing to a mountain top
- pointing round the corner on the left
- first on the right
- second on the left
- pointing at the head teacher
- pointing at their best friend
- pointing at their worst enemy
- pointing at a policeman
- pointing the way to heaven
- pointing the way to hell.

More Gestures

This activity continues the process of expressing yourself by means of your hands and facial expression.

Suitable for

KS1, KS2

Cross-curriculum link

English

Aims

- To show facial expressiveness.
- To use speech to express physical ideas.

Resources

- An open space

What to do

1. Ask them to get into pairs or groups of three and express the following by means of gesture only

   - I can smell gas. Where is it coming from?
   - Your mum's coming. Quick, let's hide.
   - I wish you'd go away.
   - Please don't tell anyone what I did.

2. When the above have been explored through gesture and facial expression you can ask the groups to use the lines as starting points for an improvisation.

3. Explain that the next activity begins with a gesture and continues into speech. The groups must improvise and create characters and a situation from the following starting points

- index finger to lips indicating silence
- thumbing a lift
- stopping someone running down the corridor
- blowing a kiss to someone
- holding your hand out to beg for money
- palm of the hand raised in a gesture of peace
- showing your fist to someone.

4. Give the groups time to rehearse the above and then the rest of the class can watch each group performing.

Dramatic Change

In this activity we learn about the shapes we can make with our bodies and how frozen posture can develop into a moving image.

Suitable for

KS1 (optional), KS2

Cross-curriculum link

PE

Aims

- To communicate meaning through body shape.
- To watch and listen to each other.

Resources

- An open space
- A drum

What to do

1. Ask the class to spread out and make dramatic changes of posture when you clap or beat a drum. Tell them to make the changes really dramatic. They must freeze and then suddenly change their posture into something completely different. Do five 'changes' of posture one after the other quickly. After several rounds of 'changes' tell them that you will call out 'action'. When you do this they must come alive in any way they like, move and speak, make sounds. The movement is suggested by the pose they find themselves in. Let them do whatever they think appropriate but ask them afterwards what they were.

2. When they have got used to changing their postures dramatically and freezing in poses, they can try the following when you call 'action'

- be an animal
- be a robot
- be a mechanical toy
- be doing a job
- be a dancer
- be a gangster.

3. Ask them now to work in pairs, one is A, the other is B. A calls out 'change' and B makes some dramatic frozen postures. When A says 'action', B must come alive in some way with a movement, speech and sound. Then B does the same with A. They can alternate like this until they become more confident.

4. Get them into groups of four or five. Ask the groups to get into a frozen pose expressing the following

- workers on strike
- a football crowd cheering
- a dramatic moment in a cricket match
- a crowd watching tennis
- aliens in their spacecraft.

After each group gets into their pose, you can call out 'action' and they must burst into life.

5. Ask them to remain in their groups but this time the frozen pose will demonstrate machines. Ask them to get into a frozen group pose to convey the following ideas, then when you call 'action' they will spring into life

- robots making a car
- a machine making jam jars
- a steam engine
- a food mixer
- a washing machine
- an electric drill
- a lawn mower
- a vacuum cleaner.

Melodrama Movement (part 1)

> **In this activity we learn about a form of theatre called Melodrama in which all movement is exaggerated.**

Suitable for

KS2

Cross·curriculum links

History, Art

Aims

- To exaggerate movement.
- To show off movement.

Resources

- A black cloak
- A false moustache

What to do

1. Look up Melodrama in a book or on the internet and find out when it was a popular form of theatre.

2. Ask the children to draw a picture of a typical melodramatic pose from the research they have done.

3. Ask the class first of all to walk normally around the room and then try the following
   - walk with head held high
   - walk proudly like a peacock
   - swagger like a hero
   - walk like a tough person
   - walk like a boxer who's won the world championship.

4. Now ask them to keep their eyes fixed on the teacher and walk up and down in a straight line doing the above movements. They must not take their eyes off you while they are moving.

5. Explain that actors in Melodrama – which was a form of theatre acting that was prevalent in the nineteenth century – hardly ever took their eyes off the audience.

6. Now explain that you are going to focus on the role of 'the villain' in Melodrama. If you have a cloak ask one of the children to put it on and stride about while the rest of the class 'hiss' and boo' at them. Explain that the convention in Melodrama was that as soon as the villain came on stage the audience would 'boo' and 'hiss'. If they have seen a pantomime they will recall how the audience reacted when a nasty person came on stage.

7. Ask them to find a picture of a villain like 'the Joker' from *Batman*, or 'Dracula' and draw a picture of him.

8. Put on the music for 'The Miraculous Mandarin' (see Appendix) and ask them to move like a villainous person. They should imagine they have a cloak that they bring up to hide their face as they move.

9. Ask them to throw back their heads and laugh in an exaggeratedly evil manner.

10. Next they find a partner. One of them is 'villain' and the other is 'victim'. They take turns at being 'villain' and 'victim'. The only sound the villain can make is an insane laugh. The only sound the 'victim' can make is a pathetic whimper. Try the following ideas

- the villain ties up the victim on a chair
- the villain ties up the victim on a railway track.

Melodrama Movement (part 2)

In this activity we continue to do activities associated with exaggerated movement in the melodramatic style of acting.

Suitable for

KS2

Cross-curriculum links

English, History

Aims

- To exaggerate movement.
- To show off movement.
- To project the voice.

What to do

1. Ask the children to exaggerate the following using mime

- I can hear something
- I can hear the sound of a distant train
- I can see the train coming in the distance
- I can see the train approaching
- I see the train passing
- I see the train disappearing into the distance.

2. Now as 'the villain' ask the children to exaggerate the following in mime

- entering as the villain
- stroking his moustache
- laughing as the villain
- enjoying being evil
- catching sight of a victim
- walking towards a victim

- capturing a victim
- tying up a victim
- throwing a victim down a hole.

3. Now they find a partner and mime the above with one of them as the 'villain' and the other as the 'victim'.

4. In their pairs they mime the following scenario in the melodramatic style of acting

- enter the villain
- the victim is watering roses
- the villain looks at the audience and strokes his moustache
- the victim continues watering
- the villain approaches slowly
- the victim suddenly sees the villain
- the villain smiles
- the victim freezes with fear
- the villain ties the victim to a chair
- the victim cries out
- the villain ties a handkerchief round the victim's mouth
- the villain takes out a big knife
- the victim sees the knife
- the villain hears something
- it is the sound of the police arriving
- the villain runs off.

5. Explain to the class that raising your right hand just before you went off stage was a convention of Melodrama. If there is a curtain in the room (an open door will do) you can ask them to practise going off and raising their right hand just beforehand. What was the purpose of this? It was to make the exit seem more dramatic, even though it seems rather silly to us now and rather funny. They can practise saying the following lines just before they exit

- Goodbye, my beloved! (then exit raising their right hand)
- Farewell, dearest Mother!
- I wish you all a fond farewell
- I take my leave of you!
- This is 'goodbye'
- I can no longer stay.

6. In pairs ask them to work on exiting and raising their right arm above their heads. Use the following lines

A: I shall never see you again. Farewell! (exit)
B: Dearest brother, farewell! (exit)

A: Remember me, William. (exit)
B: How can I forget you, Gertrude? (exit)

A & B (speaking together): We shall not meet again. Goodbye!
(exit together)

7. Still in pairs ask them to strike a tragic pose by putting the back of their hand on their forehead and saying the following in a mock tragic voice

A: Has it come to this? (hand on forehead)
B: It has indeed come to this. (hand on forehead)

A: Will you leave me destitute? (hand on forehead)
B: I have no choice, Archibald. (hand on forehead)

A: Oh no, what's to be done? (hand on forehead)
B: Nothing can be done. (hand on forehead)

Group Movement

In this activity we look at ways of synchronising movement so that a group of children all move together in the same way and at the same speed.

Suitable for

KS1, KS2

Aims

- To watch.
- To listen.
- To develop a sense of rhythm.

Cross·curriculum links

PE, Mathematics

Resources

- A CD player
- CD music from suggestions in the Appendix

What to do

1. One way of focusing the group so that they are all really concentrating is to present them with the challenge of counting 1–10 in the following ways. Ask them to stand or sit in a circle

   - all count 1–10 as a whole class
   - all count 1–10 slowly but keeping together
   - all count 1–10 quickly but keeping together
   - in two large groups count 1–10 alternately
   - in three groups count 1–10 alternately
   - in four groups count 1–10 alternately.

   When they get to 10 they start from the beginning again until you decide to stop them.

2. The above exercises should be suitable for both KS1 and KS2. The following may only be suitable for KS2. Ask the class to sit quietly in a circle. They must count from 1–10 but now only one person at a time is allowed to speak. If two people speak at the same time they must go back to 1 and start counting again. It is forbidden to count round the circle for that would be too easy. The class are not allowed to confer at any stage. This is quite a difficult exercise for this age group but will reveal a class's concentration level. You can point to a different person to start every time they have to go back to the beginning. Here is a summary of analysing concentration levels for a class

1–3 class not concentrating too well
4–5 quite good group concentration
6–8 very good group concentration
9–10 excellent group concentration.

3. In groups of three ask them to do the following together

- move together in slow motion turning 360 degrees one way and back again
- move together in slow motion turning 180 degrees and back again
- move together in slow motion turning 90 degrees and back again.

4. In groups of four they should now express the following in slow-motion movement

- a small plant growing bigger
- a fully grown plant dying back
- four daffodils growing in the sun
- four daffodils wilting in the sun
- four daffodils blown in the wind
- a tree blowing in the wind.

5. Now as individuals give them the challenge of the following ideas

- Dracula rising from the grave
- a monster waking up
- a balloon being blown up
- a football being blown up
- a rugby ball being blown up.

Variations

- In item 5 they can also work in pairs or larger groups.
- Slow music would be very effective with all of these movement exercises so look at the Appendix for some suggestions.
- When they are growing bigger and smaller you could suggest they make 'sounds' to accompany the movement.

Double-glazed Window

In this activity children learn to communicate a message through a window without the luxury of speech.

Suitable for

KS1 (optional), KS2

Cross-curriculum link

English

Aims

- To improve mime skills.
- To learn to watch others without speaking out.

Resources

- Cards on which messages have already been written
- A window frame if possible

What to do

1. Explain that double-glazed window in this drama work means that you can see people through a window of a house but cannot hear them because the double-glazing is so good.

2. Get the class into pairs and ask them to stand about six feet apart. They must imagine there is a double-glazed window between them and they cannot hear each other.

3. One of them is A and is the householder who is inside the house. B is outside the house on the pavement. B has to give A the following messages but A cannot hear because of the double-glazing. B can speak and shout as loud as they like but A cannot hear. B has to therefore 'mime' the following

- there is smoke coming out of your upstairs window
- your cat's got stuck up a tree.

4. Now ask them to swap over so that B becomes the householder and A has to communicate the following messages

- your son has kicked a ball through my window
- can I borrow a cup of sugar?

5. Now that they have got the idea the whole class can become involved in the following way. Create an area for performance where everyone can see the double-glazed window and the pavement area. Select someone from the class to be the 'householder'. That person then goes and sits in the house.

6. The rest of the class sit as the audience. One of the audience is given a card on which a message has been written. That person reads the message and, without telling anyone what it says, has to go up to the double-glazed window and try to communicate that message *through mime only* to the householder. The householder watches and after seeing the mime has to guess what the message is. Try to give everybody a turn at miming a message and also to be the householder. Here are some suggested messages, but you can prepare your own. Even better, the pupils can create their own and the teacher can be householder for one round!

- A slate has fallen from your roof and nearly killed me.
- I've come to read your gas metre.
- Your car is parked across my garage and I can't get out.
- I am the milkman. Please pay your bill.
- I am the vicar. Would you like to donate something to charity?
- Your dog has done something unmentionable in my garden.

Variations

- Try to discourage 'mouthing of words'. As much as possible must be done in gesture and movement.
- The audience must not call out. The householder has to guess. If the householder cannot understand then you can ask the audience what they think.
- In item 4 the children can make up their own messages.
- Conversely the householder can speak but the person outside the house cannot hear. This means the householder has a chance to mime.

Period Movement

In this activity we practise movement belonging to another period of history, in this case the Victorian and Edwardian periods.

Suitable for

KS1 (optional), KS2

Cross-curriculum links

History, English, Art

Aims

- To give the children a sense of history.
- To provide insight into period movement.
- To use props.

Resources

- An open space
- A set of hardback books
- Canes or walking sticks
- Top hats

What to do

1. This is a fun way of starting off period movement lessons. Have a set of books, preferably hardback, available and give the children a book each. Ask them to place the book on top of their heads and walk about in such a way that the book remains perched on the top of their heads. Explain that movement in previous periods, such as the Victorian and the Edwardian periods, was *elegant* and *stately*.

2. After five minutes or so have a competition in which each child, one at a time, walks across the room with the book perched on top of their heads. The person who manages to walk across the room without the book falling off is the winner.

3. Give them a cane to hold in their hand as they walk still with the book on their heads. Let them practise for a while before having another competition.

4. If you have top hats available (or bowler hats will do) you can now let them do movements with the hat on their head and the cane in their hand.

5. Ask the children what difference they see when someone walks with a book on their head and when they walk normally.

6. Research can be done on the internet on the Victorian and Edwardian periods regarding costumes and accessories for men and women. Objects such as canes, parasols and top hats can be drawn.

7. Get them into pairs and ask them to practise the following dialogue from *The Importance of Being Earnest* by Oscar Wilde. They should both have books on their heads

   (a) Algernon: Did you hear what I was playing, Lane?
       Lane: I didn't think it polite to listen, sir.

Explain that Algernon is the master and Lane is the butler. They both speak in very posh accents.

   (b) Lady Bracknell: You may take a seat, Mr Worthing.
       Jack: Thank you, Lady Bracknell, I prefer standing.

Explain that Lady Bracknell is seated and Jack is standing. They speak in very posh accents.

   (c) Gwendolen (looking around): Quite a charming room this is of yours, Miss Cardew.
       Cecily: So glad you like it, Miss Fairfax.

Explain that both characters are seated. They too speak in very posh accents.

8. Ask the class to write down answers to the following questions

   • What did you notice about the position of your head and neck when you moved with the book on your head?

- What did you notice about your back?
- What did you have to do when you walked with the book on your head?
- What kind of costume would the above characters be wearing?
- What accessories or props would they have with them?

9. Further work on period dialogue can be found in the scripts in Part 3 and on the website. This activity is an introduction to the concept of period movement.

Variations

- Some children will discover that having the book opened on their heads will make it easier for it to 'sit' on their heads. Allow this if you wish.
- One or two top hats will do as long as the hats sit comfortably on most children's heads. They can each have a turn at walking with the hat and cane.
- You can have a further game in which you ask the children to sit down on a chair with the book on their head and possibly stand up again.

Comedy Movement

In this activity we look at ways of moving that will create a comic effect.

Suitable for

KS1 (optional), KS2

Cross-curriculum links

Music, History, English

Aims

- To improve sense of timing.
- To respond to rhythmical patterns.

Resources

- An open space

What to do

1. Ask the class to get into groups of three and practise the following movements as a trio. They must all move, stand, sit at the same time

   - the group sits
   - the group stands
   - the group sits, crosses their legs, unfolds a newspaper and reads
   - the group stands, looks to the right, looks to the left, looks at their watches and sits
   - the group walks in, sits down, crosses their legs, folds their arms
   - the group sits, looks right, looks left, looks out front, looks surprised, stands

- sits, takes out a banana, peels it, eats it
- the group sits, thinks hard, has an idea, gets up and goes.

The children could be asked to do any combination of the above that they like and add their own comic touches.

2. Put on some jaunty music with a strong rhythm. Some aerobic exercise music is suitable for this (look at the Appendix for recommendations). The trio can now practise the following, moving together and in rhythm

- walking forward, turning left, walking forward
- walking forward, turning right, walking forward
- walking forward, turning left, walking forward, turning right, walking forward, stopping suddenly
- walking forward, opening a door, entering, walking to a table, sitting
- at the breakfast table: sit down, pick up knives and forks, eat breakfast
- at the dinner table: sit, pick up soup spoon, dip spoon into bowl, blow on it, swallow and repeat.

Allow the children to improvise and invent their own comic movements using any of the above in any combination plus adding ideas of their own.

3. Suggest now that they are going to work to do a job or play a sport. They can choose to do any of the following ideas and add their own if they wish

- sawing wood and wiping sweat from brow
- hammering in nails and hitting thumb
- taking out machine gun, firing it, being shot and dying
- climbing up a ladder, cleaning window, climbing down
- batting at the wicket, hitting the ball for six
- batting at the wicket, hitting the ball, being caught out.

4. Using facial expressions in a trio can also be a way of creating a comic effect for an audience. Try some of the following and add your own

- looking at something in the sky then it falls on your head
- walking along as a tough guy and bumping into a lamp post, looking embarrassed
- having a drink, showing that you're enjoying it, then suddenly it kills you

- laughing at someone, then getting punched on the nose
- taking a drink from someone, swallowing it, wiping your mouth, slowly realising it tastes horrible.

This kind of effect is sometimes called 'slapstick' and can be practised by individuals as well as in groups of three.

Variations

- An additional idea for item 1 would be for the trio to get out a lunch box and eat their sandwiches.

Doctor Jekyll and Mr Hyde

In this session we examine some drama ideas based on the book *Doctor Jekyll and Mr Hyde* written by Robert Louis Stevenson and look at how to incorporate the interplay of good and evil into drama, as well as providing some fun games.

Suitable for

KS1, KS2

Cross-curriculum links

English, PE

Aims

- To work as a group.
- To acquire discipline of movement.

Resources

- An open space

What to do

1. Split the class into two large groups. One group is 'Jekylls' and consists of essentially good people. The other group is 'Hydes' and consists of essentially evil people. Ask the Jekylls to get into a physical pose which will reveal their essential goodness and generosity. Ask the Hydes to get into a physical pose which will reveal their essentially evil qualities. Remember no movement. They must be like frozen statues. Go round and examine the statues. No laughing allowed.

2. Now ask the Jekylls to move/walk and do something which will express their essentially good character. The Hydes watch the Jekylls. Now ask the Hydes to move/walk in a way which will express their essentially evil character. The Jekylls watch the Hydes.

3. Ask a Jekyll to pair up with a Hyde and ask them to

- circle each other suspiciously
- prod each other
- smell each other
- shake hands with each other
- smile or glower at each other
- move away from each other as if frightened
- move in closer to each other
- ignore each other
- move away from each other
- stand at opposite ends of the room.

4. In the following game

- the Jekylls have to walk on tiptoe
- the Hydes have to crawl on the floor.

The aim of the game is for the Hydes to catch a Jekyll by the foot. As soon as a Jekyll is touched or caught by the foot he or she must become a Hyde and go down on the floor and help to catch the rest of the Jekylls so that by the end of the game everybody becomes a crawling Hyde.

Another version of this game is that as soon as a Jekyll is caught they are out of the game and must go and stand at the side or end of the room. The Hydes continue until they have caught all the Jekylls.

5. The following game is to be played using movement and sound. The aim of the game is for the Hydes to touch the Jekylls. Put the Hydes at one end of the room, and the Jekylls in the middle of the room. The Hydes make a growling sound and take one step forward towards the Jekylls and freeze. The Jekylls make a frightened sound and take three steps in any direction and freeze. If a Jekyll is touched they are out of the game and stand to one side. The game continues until all the Jekylls are caught. If anyone takes more than their allotted steps they are disqualified.

Variations

- You can ask those who are Jekylls in item 1 to change into Hydes later on.
- An alternative start to the lesson is to have a competition in which the teacher decides who is best at which role and casts them accordingly.
- In item 5 the children can have turns at being Hydes.

Visualisation

In this activity we stimulate the imagination by visualising scenes either from the real world or from imaginary places.

Suitable for

KS1, KS2

Cross-curriculum links

English, Art

Aims

- To stimulate the visual imagination.
- To use adjectives.

Resources

- An open space

What to do

1. Ask the children to sit or lie on their backs on the floor and close their eyes. You are now going to suggest a place for them to visit and they will have to describe to you at the end of each visualisation what they saw or what they heard, or both. Put on some relaxing music

   - they are at home in their bedroom
   - they are standing in the street where they live
   - they are in the school playground
   - they are at their friend's house
   - they are outside a strange house
   - they open the door and go in.

2. Now ask them to visualise some imaginary places or activities

- a deserted beach
- swimming underwater
- flying through space
- walking in the desert
- wandering in a city.

3. Ask them to write down some of the visualisations in their English books, describing what they saw as follows

- the shape and texture of what they saw
- the colours they saw
- any sounds they heard
- any people they saw
- their faces
- what they were wearing.

4. Ask them to draw some of their visualisations.

5. Now ask them to close their eyes and as soon as you say the place from the list below they must all call out what they see, one at a time, or you could ask them by name to describe what they see

- a circus
- a fairground
- a bridge
- a church
- a view from the top of a hill.

6. Tell them that you are now going to ask them to move in an environment with which they are familiar. Each person in the class works in their own space

- enter your house through the front door
- go into the kitchen
- put on the kettle
- go to your room
- check that everything is where you left it
- open the window
- go back down to the kitchen
- make yourself a cup of tea
- watch television
- start doing your homework.

7. Now tell them that you are going to take them through a landscape with which they are *not* familiar. Each child works in their own space, ignoring everyone else.

- you are lying asleep
- you wake up and find yourself on a beach
- you look around but there are no people
- you look out to sea and catch a glimpse of a boat on the horizon
- then the boat disappears
- you look behind you and see that the sand stretches out into the distance
- you look back to the sea but the sea is now sand stretching out into the distance
- you realise you are now in a desert and it is very hot
- you are boiling and sit down on the sand
- you look around but there is no one there
- you think you see what looks like a camel in the distance
- then it disappears
- you suddenly feel very sleepy
- you lie down on the sand and soon you are asleep
- you wake up
- you find you are in your own bed at home.

Variations

- They can visualise item 7 lying on their backs while you are talking to them.

Pip, Squeak and Wilfred

In this activity we have some fun games involving the above characters who were part of a comic strip in the 1920s. More can be found out about them at www.fylde.demon.co.uk/pip.htm

Suitable for

KS1, KS2

Cross-curriculum link

History

Aims

- To encourage a sense of fun.
- To encourage quick reactions.

Resources

- An open space

What to do

1. Give each person in the class a name – either Pip, Squeak or Wilfred.

2. On the command 'Go!' they move in the following way

   - Pips run around like dogs and bark
   - Squeaks move like penguins and squeak
   - Wilfreds jump like rabbits.

   On the command 'Freeze' they must all freeze. Alternatively, you can beat a drum or two pieces of wood, or play a loud piece of energetic music and stop it when you want them to stop and start it when you want them to move.

3. After practising the above so that they all understand what kind of movements they've got to make, call out either Pip, Squeak or Wilfred. If you call out 'Pip' then only the Pips move. If you call out 'Squeak' then only the Squeaks move. If you call out 'Wilfred!' only the Wilfreds move. *But if you call out 'Popski' then no one must move.* If anyone moves when you say Popski then that whole team is out. The winning team is the one that has moved only when they should move.

4. Ask them to sit in a circle. Each person must be identified as a Pip, a Squeak or a Wilfred. When you call out either 'Pip', 'Squeak' or 'Wilfred' the relevant people have to stand and run round the circle until you say 'Places'. Then they must dash round, in the same direction, until they find their place and sit down. The last person to get to their place is 'out'. At the end of this game the winners are the last Pip left, the last Squeak left and the last Wilfred left. You could have a prize for 'Chief Pip', 'Chief Squeak' and 'Chief Wilfred'.

Variations

- You could play item 3 with just the Pips, by saying 'Go' and 'Freeze'. You then have a winner who is called 'Chief Pip'. Similarly with the Squeak and Wilfred teams. These three can then compete in the 'Popski' game.

Games

In this chapter we present a collection of games featured elsewhere in the book, which can be used in a single drama session.

Suitable for

KS1, KS2

Cross-curriculum link

English

Aims

- To listen carefully.
- To acquire a sense of rhythm.

Resources

- An open space

What to do

1. This game is called 'Traffic Lights'. When you say 'Green!' everyone moves. When you say 'Red' everyone freezes. When you say 'Amber' everyone goes down on the floor. Anyone who does not do this is eliminated until there is a winner.

2. Ask the class to get in a circle. This game is called 'Imaginary Ball'. They have to throw an imaginary ball across the circle to each other and, at the same time, say the name of the person to whom they are throwing the ball. Then that person has to immediately throw the ball to someone else and say that person's name, etc. The person who hesitates or says the wrong name, or who can't think of a name or who gets muddled up is 'out' and has to sit down for the rest of the game.

The game continues until there is only one person left. That person is obviously the winner. This is a good game for the start of a lesson or for a new class to get to know each other.

3. The game 'Bing, Bong' is great fun. The children stand in a circle. You point to someone to start. That person says 'Bing', the next person says 'Bong', the next person has to say their own name. The next person says 'Bing', the next person says 'Bong', the next person says their own name and so on. It all sounds very simple but soon people begin to make mistakes and as soon as someone says the wrong thing they are 'out' and must sit down. You start again until someone else is 'out' and continue until there is a winner.

4. This game is called 'Masters and Robots'. Get the class into pairs. Each pair is a master and a robot and make a team. The robots must close their eyes and take instructions from their masters to get through a narrow gap between two chairs and then walk back to their master. The robots must have their eyes closed or have a blindfold so that they cannot see where they are going. They have to trust the masters' instructions. The instructions from the masters are as follows – 'Move forward – Move left – Move right – Stop'. If a robot so much as touches a chair they explode and are 'out'. If the robots bump into each other then both teams are out. Depending on the amount of space available it is best to have two/three teams competing at the same time. The winning pair can then compete against another winning pair and so on.

Variations

- With the game 'Bing, Bong' you can add an extra 'Bing' to make things more complicated, so that it goes 'Bing – Bong – Bing – Name'.

Use of Props

In this activity we deal with how specific props can be used for effect on stage.

Suitable for

KS1, KS2

Cross-curriculum link

English

Aims

- To learn how to use stage props for maximum effect.
- To stimulate the imagination.

Resources

- Props such as books, a comb, a mobile phone, etc. as specified

What to do

1. Using simple everyday objects is a very useful exercise to accustom children to using a prop. Ask them to use anything they have in their bag or in their pockets. The purpose is to get them to use the prop in a context that they can create themselves. They can use this exercise as a part of English. Here are some examples of how a simple prop can be 'dramatised'.

A book

Sarah enters the room and sees a book lying on the floor. She seems to recognise the book and goes over and picks it up. She looks through it and realises that it is the book she lost three months ago. What is it doing in her sister's room? She looks angry and determines to go and have it out with her sister. She storms out of the room calling out, 'Vicky!'

A comb

Emma picked up the comb and started to comb her hair. She looked into the mirror and smoothed her curls with her other hand. She wanted to look her best for the party. After all, it was her birthday and she was determined to enjoy herself. As she combed her hair she realised that the comb was not hers. Where was her comb? Had her sister borrowed it again? She was fed up with her sister borrowing her things. She ran out of the room to tell her mum.

2. In this way children can write their own context for a prop and then act it out. Other props that can be used are

   - mobile phone
   - watch
   - scarf
   - pen/pencil
   - school bag.

   Basically anything that pupils use on a daily basis can be 'contextualised' and then used in a short drama scene.

3. The following props are always useful to collect and store in a props cupboard to be used in Drama lessons

   - walking sticks/canes
   - umbrellas/parasols
   - gloves
   - hats
   - brooms
   - binoculars
   - spectacles
   - plastic cups, plates, etc.

   A quick visit to a charity shop is an inexpensive way of gathering props for the drama props cupboard. Sometimes opticians will give you spare spectacle frames.

4. As part of their English lessons children could write a short piece that focuses on a prop and then the class can act out some of the scenes in Drama lessons. Here are some examples of the way a prop can be used in English and Drama.

A broom

Cinderella picked up her broom and started to sweep the floor as her sisters had instructed her. She was always the one who did the housework. Her sisters did nothing. She swept thoroughly because on many occasions her sisters had insisted that she do the sweeping again if they weren't satisfied.

Gloves

Oliver was cold. He was shivering. He looked around the room, which was dark and full of coffins. He looked at the miserable fire, which was going out. He remembered that he had a pair of gloves – but where were they? He looked in his trouser pockets but they were not there. Where had he left them? Had they dropped out of his pockets? Or had they been stolen by Noah? Then he remembered his coat hanging on a peg by the door. He looked in the pockets and there they were! He put them on quickly and went and lay down in the coffin that was to be his bed.

Variations

- In item 1 you could ask a pair of children to improvise on what Sarah says to Vicky or what Emma says to her sister.
- In item 4, the 'A broom' groups of three can improvise on how the two ugly sisters treat Cinderella and in 'Gloves' pairs can improvise on how Noah treats Oliver.

Crowd Work

In this activity the whole class works together as a crowd or a part of a crowd.

Suitable for

KS1, KS2

Cross-curriculum link

English

Aims

- To listen.
- To work with many people at the same time.

Resources

- An open space

What to do

1. Ask the children to stand in a circle and close their eyes. They are to start humming gently, increase the volume and then decrease the volume. They increase and decrease the volume by listening to each other.

2. Now ask them to do the same thing but this time they raise their arms above their heads as they increase the volume and lower their arms as they decrease the volume. Do this several times until they get used to all working together as one. They should still have their eyes shut.

3. Now with their eyes open ask them to point to the centre of the circle and make the humming sound. As the sound increases in volume they walk into the centre of the circle, still pointing, and as it decreases in volume they walk backwards to where they started from. Working like this as a whole class needs lots of concentration from everybody.

4. Still with their eyes open and pointing to the centre of the circle they move in, but this time all point upwards as they reach the centre of the circle – as if they are pointing to an object in the sky. Then they move backwards slowly to where they started, still pointing upwards. They should all be pointing upwards in the same direction.

5. Ask the class to bunch up as a crowd all facing in the same direction. Tell them they've all got to look up together and point at something in the sky – all at the same time.

6. Now one of them shouts 'Look!' and points somewhere else. All the class look in that direction. Another person shouts 'Look!' and the class look in that direction. Try this with a number of people shouting 'Look!' and the class responding by looking in the direction in which they point.

7. Now ask them to form a line, all facing the same direction. They are spectators at a tennis match. On the beat of a drum or a handclap from you the crowd look one way and then the other as if following the tennis ball.

Variations

- Sometimes children respond more positively with an 'aah' sound instead of a humming sound.

Using the Five Senses

In this activity we experiment with the five senses and create a scenario involving humans and alien creatures.

Suitable for

KS1, KS2

Cross-curriculum link

English

Aims

- To work with a partner.
- To work in a group.
- To work in a large group.
- To concentrate.

Resources

- An open space

What to do

1. Ask the children to freeze in the pose of someone
   - listening
   - watching
   - tasting
   - smelling
   - touching.

2. Now develop this into a more detailed approach. Ask them to use their facial expressions for the following
   - eavesdropping at a door
   - looking at a storm cloud
   - tasting something unpleasant

- smelling a nice smell
- touching something rough.

3. Using the five senses is an important part of drama movement so give them some more challenging situations involving the five senses

- listening at a door behind which someone is saying unpleasant things about them
- listening to someone praising them
- listening as if they don't understand
- listening as if they can't believe what is being said
- listening for spooky sounds in a deserted house

- watching a horse race where their horse is winning
- watching a football match where their team is losing
- looking at an aeroplane landing and then crashing
- watching a comedy programme on TV
- staring at their school report, which is terrible

- biting and tasting a beefburger
- tasting an unpleasant medicine
- licking a delicious ice cream
- sucking on a lollypop
- drinking and tasting their favourite drink

- sniffing a burning smell
- smelling a perfumed candle
- smelling their favourite food being cooked
- smelling something foul
- smelling something they can't identify

- stroking a cat
- warming their hands at the fire
- touching something smooth
- touching a brick wall
- touching an elephant's skin.

4. Divide the class into two. Half are aliens and half are humans on the aliens' planet. There is a solid wall in between them so that they cannot see each other. Give the groups the following sensory ideas with which to experiment

- the humans approach the wall and listen carefully
- the aliens approach the wall and listen
- the humans smell something
- the aliens smell something
- the humans try to look over the wall but fail
- the aliens try to look over the wall and fail
- the humans see slime on the wall and taste it
- the aliens smell the humans and look forward to tasting them
- the humans feel the wall to see if they can break it down
- the aliens hide behind a rock on their side of the wall
- the humans break down the wall
- the aliens stand up and the humans run off screaming because they are so ugly!

5. Try the above scenario with sound. The humans can speak but the aliens can only make sounds. The aliens hear them but cannot understand what they say.

6. Give the aliens the following challenges to rehearse

- they can 'see' with the palms of their hands
- they can taste with their stomachs
- they can 'smell' with their eyes.

The humans can be given the following challenges

- they are astronauts in spacesuits
- they can only move in slow motion
- their speech is distorted.

7. After rehearsing some or all of the above there should be at least a ten-minute sequence that the children can present as a piece of drama. Suitable music should be used to accompany the action (see Appendix for suggestions).

Changing Shapes

This activity deals with physically changing shape from one type of person to another.

Suitable for

KS1, KS2

Cross-curriculum links

Music, English, PE

Aims

- To loosen up the joints of the body.
- To communicate ideas through posture.

Resources

- An open space

What to do

1. Ask the children to spread out and find a space by themselves where they won't bump into anybody. Put on some slow music if possible and say that they are going to transform themselves from one kind of character to another. Ask them to move in slow motion to echo the music. Try the following first of all

   - twist the body into contorted shapes in slow motion.

   They keep moving until they freeze in the following shape

   - an evil devil.

   Now they carry on moving until they freeze in the shape of

   - an angel.

Now they continue to move from one shape to another

- devil – angel
- angel – devil.

Or if you like

- a good person
- an evil person.

2. Once they get used to moving slowly from one shape to another give them the following opposite characters to try

  - fat person – thin person
  - tall person – short person
  - smart-looking person – tramp
  - shy person – loud person (introvert – extrovert).

3. Try animals now in the same way. Change from

  - cat to giraffe
  - fish to tortoise
  - dragon to cuckoo.

4. Now they should try going from human to animal and back again

  - princess to mermaid
  - batman to eagle
  - wizard to swan
  - witch to chicken
  - hero to lion
  - Harry Potter to snake.

Variations

- If the children find item 3 difficult give them a chance to portray the animals without transforming them until they have a clear idea of what they are aiming for.

Movement and Voice

In this activity we prepare for Part 2 by doing a lot of movement in which the voice is an integral part of the action.

Suitable for

KS1, KS2

Cross-curriculum link

PE

Aims

- To integrate movement and voice.
- To develop a sense of rhythm in tandem with a partner.

Resources

- An open space

What to do

1. Ask the class to move in the following ways
   - with small steps
   - with long strides
   - with short sideways steps
   - bouncing up and down
   - leaping forward with both feet
   - tiptoeing.
2. Now ask them to make a sound with every movement they have made above.

3. Next ask them to make the following simultaneous movements and sounds
- walk and grunt on each step
- step and squeak on each step
- walk forward and make a ferocious sound on each step as if they were giants
- creep on tiptoe as if they don't want to be heard and make an appropriate sound on each step.

4. Now they walk forward with a partner and every so often stop, look around and make a shushing sound.

5. Next they walk forward with their partner, speaking the following lines together as they walk

Fi, Fi, Fo, Fum, I smell the blood of an English man

Be he alive or be he dead

I'll grind his bones to make my bread.

6. They repeat this with their partner, this time inserting some dramatic pauses to make an impact.

7. Then they try the following nursery rhyme, moving and speaking together and then inserting some dramatic pauses

Mary had a little lamb

Its feet were white as snow

And everywhere that Mary went

The lamb was sure to go.

8. In the same way, recite the following nursery rhyme *alternately* while moving:

Pussycat, pussycat, where have you been?

I've been to London to see the Queen!

Pussycat, pussycat,

What did you there?

I frightened a little mouse under a chair!

Part 2
Voice

Voice

I have always found that speech is far more difficult to teach than movement so, to begin with, I like to explore the possibilities of sound rather than speech. Speaking and singing – without necessarily being a singer – can also be an icebreaker and can lead to some very interesting drama sessions where pupils really learn to enjoy their voices in a very uninhibited manner. It is also important, I feel, to encourage group awareness by using choral speech and repetition using poems as well as plays. Many of the activities in this book rely on a sense of the group all working together towards the same end rather than on individuals showing off – though there will always be the exhibitionists who must be encouraged to listen and the shy ones who must be encouraged to come forward.

Sing Up!

In this activity pupils learn to experiment with their voices and communicate by singing words as well as speaking them. It is great fun once you get used to it but a good singing voice is not necessary at all.

Suitable for

KS2

Cross-curriculum links

English, Music

Aims

- To learn to speak with articulation.
- To learn how to project the voice.
- To acquire self-confidence in speech.
- To learn the range of the voice.
- To take chances.
- To have a positive attitude.
- To work with others creatively.

Resources

- Your own voice and an open mind are all that is necessary
- Any space, but the larger the better

What to do

1. Ask the class to sit in a circle. In order to achieve a perfect circle ask them either to touch fingertips or touch elbows.
2. Go round the circle and ask each person to say his or her name as clearly as possible, one at a time.

3. Explain that you now require each person to speak their name in the following ways

- loudly
- quietly
- shouting it
- in a whisper
- stressing the first letter
- stressing the last letter
- speaking the first vowel
- pronouncing all the vowels in the word
- pronouncing all the consonants in the word
- speaking your name normally.

4. Now tell the class that they will have to *sing* their own name when it comes to their turn, as if introducing themselves to the rest of the class. Each person must stand when they introduce themselves.

5. Once everybody has had a go at introducing themselves they can add the following details about themselves, still in singing mode

- their age
- their school
- their favourite subjects at school
- their worst subjects at school
- their favourite teacher.

6. Ask the class to get into pairs and rehearse a *singing conversation* about any of the following subjects

- what they got for their birthday or for Christmas
- a description of their parents or their brothers or sisters
- what they did during the holidays.

Variations

- You can introduce a bit of variety into this session by having a memory name game at either the beginning or in the middle of the lesson as follows. Ask them all to close their eyes and name
  - the person on their right
  - the person on their left

- the fifth person on their right
- the person opposite, etc.

- Pronouncing vowels and consonants separately from the same word helps articulation and projection. You can ask them to separate the vowels and consonants from
  - their own name
  - your name
  - the school name
  - their best friend's name
  - their favourite book's title.

- As a variation the speaking of the names can be done by alternating 'loudly' and 'quietly', so that as you go round the circle the first person says their name loudly, the second quietly and so on.

Witch Voice?

This activity is devoted to vocal preparation work for *Macbeth*. It is an ideal introduction to Shakespeare and the way words can communicate meaning through sound.

Suitable for

KS2

Cross-curriculum link

English

Aims

- To achieve clear articulation.
- To project the voice with confidence.
- To enjoy the sound of language.

Resources

- An open space is preferable but this session could be done at the children's desks
- Fourteen cards, each containing one word from the witch's chant from *Macbeth*. Make as many cards as there are children in your class.

  Fair is foul, and foul is fair:
  Hover through the fog and filthy air.

- Paper and pens or pencils

What to do

1. Ask the children to describe a witch.
2. Ask them to draw their version of a witch.

3. Ask each of them to make a 'witch sound'.

4. Ask them to add a gesture and a facial expression to their 'witch sound'.

5. Now give out the cards containing the chant from *Macbeth*.

6. Each child should have a word in front of them.

7. Ask each child to pronounce their word out loud.

8. Ask each child to say their word in the following way
- mysteriously
- in a whisper
- in a high voice
- in a low voice.

9. Now you say the chant in the right order from the text and the children stand up when they hear their word.

10. Say the chant again, and this time each child goes and stands in the correct order of the chant.

11. Each child now speaks their word in the right order.

12. Now ask each child to pronounce their word in the following ways
- slowly
- quickly
- clearly
- mumbling.

13. Ask the whole class to speak the chant, keeping together.

14. Now ask them to speak the chant as a whole class
- on their knees
- on their bellies
- on their backs
- crouching.

15. By this time most of the class will know the chant by heart. Ask if anyone would like to perform the chant in front of the rest of the class on their own.

16. Put them into groups and ask them to rehearse the chant as a group and then each group can perform in front of the others.

Variations

- You could suggest in the group chant that they be
  - moving around a pot
  - passing a mysterious object to each other
  - swaying backwards and forwards or from side to side
  - whispering the whole thing.
- The following voice suggestions could also enhance the quality of the communication
  - as if they are very old
  - as if they are all blind
  - as if they are young children.
- To finish off you could ask them if they would like to do a comedy version of the chant by adding some improvised words or actions.

Sound Effects (part 1)

> In this activity the class will work together to experiment with sounds in order to enjoy using their voices.

Suitable for

KS1, KS2

Cross-curriculum link

English

Aims

- To make sounds with the voice.
- To communicate meaning with sounds.
- To work with others.
- To listen more actively.

Resources

- An open space where the children can sit comfortably on the floor in a circle
- It is preferable that no ties be worn for this kind of drama work

What to do

1. Ask the group to sit in a circle.
2. Ask them to think of a sound and then make that sound with their voices.

   You could suggest some examples, such as

   - a creaking door
   - a windy night
   - thunder
   - a distant train.

3. Go round the circle and ask each person to make their sound.

4. Then go round the circle again and this time *the whole group must repeat* the sound that the first person makes.

5. In the same way go round the circle again, but this time be more specific by asking each person to make the following sounds

- an animal sound
- a monster sound
- a robot sound
- a machine sound
- a kung fu sound
- war-chant sounds
- football-ground chanting.

6. As before, go round the circle and the whole group repeats the sound made by the first person.

7. Now ask them to make any sound they like and add a gesture with their hands to accompany the sound.

8. Get them into groups of three/four and ask each group to create a machine, with each person in the group making sounds and movements. Be sure to remind them of the purpose of their machine.

Variations

- Instead of going round the circle consecutively, the children could point to any person to make the next sound.
- They could try making the sounds standing instead of sitting.
- You could play a 'muted sounds' game in which the children make quiet sounds accompanied by gesture and movement and the class have to guess what the sound is.

Sound Effects (part 2)

> Here the children will continue to use their voices to make sounds but work increasingly with others to create sound effects.

Suitable for

KS1 (optional), KS2

Cross-curriculum link

English

Aims

- To listen carefully.
- To keep together.
- To project the voice.

Resources

- An open space where the whole class can sit in a circle
- Ties should not be worn

What to do

1. At the start of the lesson ask the children to do the following enjoyable exercises in order to loosen their voices

   - open your mouth as wide as you can
   - make your mouth as small as you can
   - stick out your tongue
   - waggle your tongue in your mouth
   - give me a smile
   - smile with your teeth closed
   - waggle your nose
   - open your mouth and go 'aahhh'

- say 'boo'
- say 'boo' as fast as you can
- pronounce the letter 'k'
- make the sound 'ka'
- make the sound 'ka' as fast as you can.

2. Tell the class that they are all going to make sounds together, keeping together. Let them try the following sounds together

- aaaaaaaaaa
- baaaaaaaaaa
- eeeeeeeeeee
- laaaaaaaaaaa
- iiiiiiiiiiiiiiii
- babababababa
- ooooooooo
- lalalalalala
- uuuuuuuuu
- kakakakakaka.
- hmmmmmm

3. Now the class must make sounds together but alter the *volume* from loud to quiet and quiet to loud. Try the above sounds – you act as conductor.

4. They should join hands in a circle and imagine the following passing through every single person in the circle

- an electric current
- a thunderbolt
- a Mexican wave
- an icy wind.

5. Each of the above can be accompanied by an appropriate sound going round the circle.

6. Ask them to get into groups of three/four and create the atmosphere of the following through the use of sound and movement

- trees blowing in the wind
- a snake pit
- a train station
- one of their own choosing.

7. Ask the class to improvise on the following ideas using one or two of the group as the 'sound effects person'

- two people are having a romantic evening at a restaurant with musical sound effects in the background
- you are watching a 'horror film' on TV and being really scared by the music and the sound effects
- you are dreaming that you are getting your own back on your least favourite teacher.

Variations

- In group work you could divide the group into two: humans, and objects who make the sound effects.
- In the electric current work, as a variation, the current could go in different directions as long as there is only one current being passed through the circle.
- To increase and decrease volume the teacher could stand in the middle of the circle and raise and lower their arms or, better still, the pupils could take turns at being conductor.

Playing with Words

In this activity we learn to experiment with words and then put them into story form.

Suitable for

KS1 (optional), KS2

Cross-curriculum link

English

Aims

- To pronounce words clearly.
- To enjoy the sound of words.
- To place words in a sequence.
- To make up a story.

Resources

- These exercises could be done at desks but an open space is preferable
- A notebook or paper and pencil

What to do

1. Ask the children to write down a word of one syllable. Give them a few examples, such as

    - man
    - sun
    - tree.

2. Ask each person in turn to pronounce their word clearly.

3. Now ask them to write down any word of two syllables. Examples could be

    - city
    - balloon
    - prosper.

4. Now ask each person in turn to pronounce their word clearly and then to say it in two parts. For example ci – ty, ball – oon, pros – per.

5. Ask them now to write down a word of three syllables, for example
- thunderbolt
- poverty.
- management

6. Ask them each to pronounce their word as one and then in three parts, separating each syllable. For example thun – der – bolt.

7. Now ask them to make up a sentence using all their words in the same sentence and it has to make sense. Each child reads out their sentence.

An example of a sentence could be 'A man was walking through a city when he was suddenly struck by a thunderbolt.'

8. The next sequence is to ask the class to read their sentences out loud in the following way as if telling a story
- quietly
- dramatically
- mysteriously
- to a crowd of a thousand people.

9. Ask the class to get into groups of three/four and to put all their sentences together to make sense and create a story.

Variations

- If a group has an interesting story to tell one of the group could read out the story while the others mime it.
- The stories could be longer than four sentences and another group could volunteer to mime it.
- One of the group could volunteer to make sound effects.
- Another variation game on this theme could be for you to give each group a series of words and the group has to make up a story from it. For example
  - bear – forest – bleeding – save
  - sweets – mother – sick – hospital
  - home – treasure – tunnel – collapse
  - spaceship – toolbag – rescue – captain
  - spin – trolley – steal – police.

Nonsense Words

In this activity we continue to work on vocalising words but now we make up our own nonsense words!

Suitable for

KS1, KS2

Cross-curriculum link

English

Aims

- To invent words.
- To convey meaning.

Resources

- Paper and pen/pencil
- An open space

What to do

1. Revise thinking of real words with one, two and three syllables as in the last activity.
2. Ask the children to make up a nonsense word that does not make sense. For example
   - booloogoo
   - kaneestometa
   - blubberstock
   - finkeevoo.
3. Go round the class and ask each child to say their word and then the rest of the class repeat it.

4. Choose some of the words that the children offer and ask everyone in the group to say the nonsense word as if it means something. For example

- point to something in the room and say the word
- point to someone and say the word
- point to a part of your body and say the word.

5. Now get them working in pairs or threes and ask them to make up a conversation in nonsense language about the following activities

- a visit to the dentist
- cleaning dirty windows
- arriving late at school
- having a bath.

6. Now ask them in their groups to make up an advert on TV for a product of their choosing but they can only talk in nonsense language.

7. Set up a family situation where the parents talk in nonsense language and the child cannot understand what they are saying!

Variations

- Rehearsal is necessary before performances take place in this kind of work so be sure to give them plenty of time to think and practise.
- Pair work could be done here by setting up the following situations as a preparation for group work. One of the pair has to explain to the other in nonsense words
  - what they had for breakfast
  - what they got for their birthday
  - who their favourite singer is and why.

Repetition and Variation

In this activity children are taught to think about the vocal variations that are possible when saying simple words and sentences.

Suitable for

KS1, KS2

Cross-curriculum link

English

Aims

- To introduce vocal variation.
- To use volume.
- To use tone.
- To use pitch.

Resources

- An open space

What to do

1. Ask the class to sit in a circle and then do a few voice exercises. All the class together pronounce the following sounds sharply

  - boo!
  - coo!
  - doo!
  - foo!
  - goo!
  - loo!

  - moo!
  - poo!
  - shoo!
  - voo!
  - woo!

2. Now go through the same words again but this time ask one of the class to start and then go round the circle with the next person saying the word in a different way – either in a different tone, volume, accent or intensity.

3. Now do the same kind of thing but this time using common, everyday words. Try to get them to think about the meaning of saying a simple word in different ways

   - No
   - Yes
   - Please
   - Really
   - Come on
   - Why?
   - Where?
   - When?
   - How?

4. Now try common sentences to be pronounced in various ways. Remind them about the possibilities of stressing different words

   - Where are you?
   - What did you say?
   - I'm going out.
   - Mum says I can.
   - Take that chewing gum out of your mouth.
   - Don't make me say it.

5. In pairs ask them to make up variations for the following sentences. The second person has to 'make up' an answer

   - Did you go to the pictures last night?
   - I'm going to tell mum about you.
   - Why are you spending so long on your homework?
   - Who was that I saw you talking to?
   - Tell me the answer.

Newspaper Headlines

We deal with newspaper headlines in this session and how we can convert them into drama involving a whole range of characters and situations.

Suitable for

KS1 (optional), KS2

Cross-curriculum links

English, History, Art

Aims

- To make pupils aware of the importance of news items.
- To understand the difference between rumour and truth.
- To understand some journalistic techniques.

Resources

- Copies of some daily newspapers
- Pencil and paper

WHAT TO DO

1. Ask the pupils to get into groups of four. Ask them to react to the following news by discussing the matter as a group and making up a scene in which more and more rumours are added to the story

   - news that your school is going to close because of flooding
   - news that two pupils have disappeared after a school trip
   - news that the headmaster and several staff have gone down with a mystery bug
   - news that someone saw two rats scuttling across the playground

- news that the Queen is coming to visit the school
- news that the world will end on 21 December according to the Mayan calendar.

2. Now ask the groups to select one member to be a reporter who interviews the others about any or all of the above stories. Other characters can be

   - headmaster
   - deputy headmaster
   - a parent
   - a teacher from the school
   - a rat infestation officer
   - secretary to the Queen.

3. Give each group paper and pencil and ask them to write down a newspaper headline for each of the above news items.

4. Now ask each group to pretend they are old-fashioned newspaper sellers who used to call out headlines on street corners. Each person in the group selects a headline from the ones they have created and goes round the class shouting it out and urging people to buy their newspaper.

5. Ask the groups to create a freeze-frame photograph of each of the above news items which will be featured in the newspaper. One of the group reads out a headline for the picture.

6. Read out or photocopy the following news item and give it to each group.

   ITV is to celebrate 30 years of its children's programming by screening classic TV shows for two days next month.

   Programmes including

   Rainbow
   Super Gran
   Press Gang
   The Raggy Dolls
   Children's Ward

   will all be broadcast.

   Digital channel CITV will clear its schedule on 5 and 6 January to screen almost nine hours of old favourites each day.

Other popular shows to be screened include

Count Duckula
Art Attack
The Tomorrow People
Puddle Lane
Rosie and Jim.

7. Ask the children to write down on a piece of paper their favourite TV programme and the reasons why they like it. Then they should join up with others who liked the same programme and present an extract from the show.

War Chants

> In this activity children are shown how powerful sounds and words can be when used in a repetitive manner.

Suitable for

KS2

Cross-curriculum links

English, Music

Aims

- To work as a group.
- To focus and concentrate.
- To develop a sense of rhythm.

Resources

- An open space

What to do

1. Ask the children to sit in a circle and then ask them to think of clapping a simple rhythm. Tell them not to make it too long. Give them an example of what you mean and then let each child clap a rhythm.

2. This time as each child claps a rhythm the whole class repeats the rhythm, all clapping together.

3. When they are used to this way of working ask them to go faster round the circle.

4. Now ask them to stand up and in the next round of clapping they must add stamping with their feet. In the same way the circle repeats whatever clapping rhythm or stamping rhythm is started by an individual.

5. Now ask them to add a word or a sound to the clapping and stamping rhythms. Again everyone repeats what the first person started. Give them the idea of an aggressive war chant.

6. Ask them to get into groups of no more than five. Each group must find a clapping, stamping rhythm accompanied by a word or a sound. It will be easier if they think of the sounds as being like an aggressive war chant.

7. Watch each group individually to see what they come up with.

8. Now ask them to add movement to their repetitions. Again give them the idea of an aggressive war chant.

Variations

- At the end of the session, once they have become adept at war chant repetitions, you could have a game in which the most aggressive group are the winners.
- You could pit two groups against each other getting closer and closer. Stop them before they leap on each other!

Once Upon a Time (part 1)

In this activity children learn to tell stories and then have them enacted by the group.

Suitable for

KS1, KS2

Cross-curriculum link

English

Aims

- To speak clearly.
- To speak and move as a specific character.
- To use the imagination.

Resources

- Pencil and paper
- An open space (optional)

What to do

1. The children could either be at their desks with pencil and paper or in the drama studio sitting on the floor.

2. Ask them to write a story beginning 'Once upon a time there was ...' They must think of a person, an animal, an object – anything they like – who is going to be the main character of their story.

3. Ask them to sit in a circle with their papers and then ask anyone to start reading their story. When the reader comes to the subject of their story they must point to someone in the class. For example if they say 'Once upon a time there was a prince ...', they must point to someone in the class to be 'the prince'. That person must then stand up and walk and speak a sentence like a prince.

4. Give as many people as possible the opportunity to read out their introductory sentence and choose someone to be their main character.

5. No one can be chosen twice to be a main character so that as many children as possible get the opportunity to 'act out' a character.

6. After everyone has had a go ask them to continue writing their story by adding a descriptive word – an adjective – to their main character. For example

- once upon a time there was a happy prince ....
- once upon a time there was an old king ...
- once upon a time there was a wily fox ...
- once upon a time there was a tin soldier ...

7. Again the storyteller must point to someone in the class who will 'enact' their main character. It can be the same person as before or someone different but the same rule applies in that everyone can only have one go as the main character of a story.

8. Now ask the children to add an action to their story. For example

- once upon a time there was a happy prince who when he woke up in the morning sang a happy song ...
- once upon a time there was an old king who was so old that he staggered to get to his throne ...
- once upon a time there was a wily fox who used to look over the farmer's fence and eye all the lovely chickens ...
- once upon a time there was a tin soldier who used to march very stiffly and bump into walls ...

9. Again ask the storytellers to read out their story clearly and choose an 'actor' to enact their main character with voice and movement. The 'actor' can make up sentences and start to speak appropriately as the main character as well as moving in a specific way.

Once Upon a Time (part 2)

In this activity children continue to build on the stories they have created and select more 'actors' to act out their ideas.

Suitable for

KS1, KS2

Cross-curriculum links

English, Music

Aims

- To write with imagination.
- To have an ear for dialogue.
- To use descriptive language.
- To act with the voice.

Resources

- Pen and paper

What to do

1. The children can now be allowed to continue writing their stories and introduce another character in the storyline. Give them time to think about who their second character might be but remind them of the importance of descriptive words – adjectives – and actions that are not impossible for an actor to imitate. Give them this as an example

   - Once upon a time there was a happy prince who sang a joyful song every day when he woke up in the morning. He used to wake up the whole neighbourhood with his singing, especially the grumpy old Baron who lived next door to the palace. The old Baron used to cover his ears with his pillow but the prince sang so loudly that he was forced to mutter and get up …

- Once upon a time there was an old king who was so old that he used to stagger up to his throne. The queen, his wife, who was much younger than him used to help him to sit on his throne but the king did not like to be helped and often cursed at his wife for helping him …

2. In the same way as in the last activity ask each storyteller to select two actors who will enact his story. The actors must invent their own dialogue and imitate the movement of the characters as explained in the story.

3. The storyteller must now write some speeches for the two characters, so time must be allowed for this before returning to the 'acting area'

- Once upon a time there was a happy prince who sang a joyful song every time he woke up in the morning. Unfortunately the grumpy old Baron who lived next door to the palace used to curse and swear because he could not have a lie in.
'I'm fed up with that little prince', the Baron used to mutter 'if he continues to sing in the morning like this I'm going to have to do something about it.'
The prince was oblivious to everything and sang his song quite happily every morning with these words

  'My song is a song of joy
  Because I'm a happy boy.
  The sun rises and I'm glad,
  I never feel sad
  Because I'm a happy boy
  My song always brings joy.'

4. You should now ask them to get into groups of three to work on their stories. Each storyteller can then have two actors who will speak and enact the characters.

5. Ask them to make a clear distinction between when the storyteller speaks and when the characters do actions and speak. This must be 'planned' in advance before any performance in front of an audience can take place.

6. When a group thinks they are ready to have their stories enacted the whole class can sit round and watch.

7. Build up the stories slowly and do not be tempted to let the children rush to finish their stories. Check the writing of the stories as the children compose them and make suggestions as to (especially) descriptive words that can then be translated into character in performance. For example

- a melancholy clown
- a pompous giant
- a browbeaten slave
- an adventurous explorer
- a sinister fortune teller
- a musical snake charmer
- an energetic acrobat
- a courageous lion tamer
- an oily devil
- a shrivelled old professor
- a magnificent magician
- a ruthless gangster.

Character Voices (part 1)

In this activity children learn how to experiment with and imitate character voices and gain confidence in projecting their accents and tones.

Suitable for

KS2

Cross-curriculum link

English

Aims

- To improve sense of timing.
- To adopt a character quickly.
- To experiment with accents.

Resources

- An open space

What to do

1. Ask the class to walk around the room continuously and look at other people's feet. When you clap your hands the children must freeze and stand still, looking at the nearest pair of feet. Then they look up into the person's eyes and say, as if with big surprise

   - Goodness! It's you!

2. Do the same again and on the handclap, they freeze and say the following with great surprise to the person whose feet are closest to them. They may wish to shake their hand

   - Why, it's you, again!
   - I never thought to see you here!

- Who are you?
- I don't believe it!
- Well, well, fancy seeing you here!

3. Walk around the room looking at the floor but as they pass people they look into their eyes and then back at the floor again. This time on the handclap, they freeze, hold it for five seconds, then go back and speak to the last person whose eyes they looked at and say

- Don't I know you from somewhere?

They can continue the conversation if they like.

4. Do the same again and this time on the handclap they go back and speak to the person they last looked at and say their name as if they have just recognised them

- Why, it's ... do you remember me?

They continue the conversation for as long as they can.

5. Now they join with a partner and do the same as above, this time having a longer improvised conversation with their partner, which can be rehearsed and then performed in front of the class. It could go something like this

Why, it's Walter Jones, isn't it?
Yes, you're Bert Jenkins, aren't you?
That's right. I haven't seen you for years.
We were at school together!
That's right – all those years ago.
What are you doing now?
(And continue.)

6. This time in pairs they imagine they are a couple of elderly pensioners walking down the street in opposite directions. As they pass they seem to recognise each other. They stop and have a conversation. They should walk and talk as old people. They should remember to consider the following ideas when creating their character voice

- they may be a bit deaf
- they may have false teeth
- they may use a walking stick.

7. This time in their pairs they are a couple of gangsters who used to work together. They remember each other as they pass and start to talk about the old days. They may like to consider the following ideas for movement and voice

   - they walk with a swagger
   - they wear a hat
   - they may have an American accent
   - they are very tough
   - they gesture with their hands a lot.

8. Once they have established their characters and rehearsed their improvised dialogues you may like to ask each pair to perform their favourite scene in front of the rest of the class.

Character Voices (part 2)

In this activity children continue to experiment with their voices as vehicles for character.

Suitable for

KS2

Cross-curriculum link

English

Aims

- To use an accent/voice to complement a specific character.
- To encourage confidence by playing broad types of character.
- To work with a partner.
- To develop the confidence to act in front of others.
- To play a character without laughing.

Resources

- An open space with a stage area (optional)
- Some props to aid character work

What to do

1. Everyone walks around the room in the following ways

   - as if carrying a very heavy object
   - as if driving a sports car
   - as if driving a tractor
   - as if feeding chickens
   - as if milking a cow.

2. Now they should all walk slowly around the room and scratch their heads as if they've forgotten something. They have to think of an object then remember what it was, go back and get it and if possible use it. They then perform the action in front of the class.

3. All walk round the room slowly and thoughtfully as if they've forgotten something then, suddenly remembering (facial expression), they have to say what it was they forgot. The character they are playing is rather slow and a bit stupid. Start them off with the following ideas and then they can move on to their own

   - (as a farmer) Ooo-aarr! I forgot to milk my cows.
   - (a pupil) Oooo! I can't remember … Oh, yes, I forgot to bring my books to school.

4. Now ask individuals in the class if they'd like to invent another slow-witted character who has forgotten something and they have to perform it in front of the class. Any character, any accent, any object they've forgotten.

5. Now our slow-witted characters should have an accent of some kind. They join with a partner and work on the idea of two slow-witted characters meeting in the following circumstances

   - waiting to see the doctor
   - waiting for a train
   - waiting in a queue to see a film
   - waiting for the cows to come home.

Character Voices (part 3)

In this activity we are going to consider acting 'posh' people and finding voices and movement to match. This activity can be linked to the scripted section from *A Christmas Carol* in Part 3.

Suitable for

KS2

Cross-curriculum link

English

Aims

- To learn to match a voice to a specific character.
- To act larger than life.

Resources

- An open space with a stage area (optional)
- Some optional props such as top hats, canes, white gloves, monocles

What to do

1. Ask the class to walk around the room in the following contrasted ways
   - stiffly and then floppily
   - proudly and then humbly
   - happily and then unhappily
   - smiling and then depressed
   - looking down on people and looking up to people.
2. Now the whole class walk around the room as posh people. As they pass others they address them with as posh a voice as they can, using the following phrases
   - Good morning.
   - Top of the morning to you!

- How are you?
- Nice to see you.
- How's the family?

3. Now they walk around the room as ignorant, uneducated people with a very 'rough' accent. As they pass others they can say the following greetings in an appropriate accent

- Allo!
- Cheers, mate!
- 'ow yer doing?
- All right?

4. Now they find a partner and repeat the above 'walks', alternating the characters so that they both have a go at playing all the characters.

5. Ask the pairs to devise a little scene in which one of them is a 'posh' person and the other is a poor – but not aggressive – beggar on a street corner. The following ideas could be put forward

- The posh person
  - speaks and walks in a very upright manner
  - looks down on people.
- The beggar is
  - cold and weary
  - dressed shabbily
  - smelly.

6. They can change partners now or stay with the same partner and this time they are both going to be 'posh' people. They must try to retain their accent. They can discuss the following topics together

- what you bought your family for Christmas
- what you bought yourself for Christmas
- what you bought for the poor people living in your area.

Character Voices (part 4)

This activity develops work begun in the activity on page 184. It gives children the opportunity to think about which voice best suits a character and to experiment further with accent and tone.

Suitable for

KS1 (optional), KS2

Cross-curriculum link

English

Aims

- To widen the range of character voices.
- To project the voice.

What to do

1. Ask the class to mime what they think the following characters do

   - a hairdresser
   - a teacher
   - a secretary
   - a traffic warden
   - a magician

   - a postman
   - a waitress
   - a fortune teller
   - a cleaner
   - a priest.

2. Now ask the class to speak a typical sentence the above character types might say. You could ask them to write it down first.

3. Ask them to choose a partner and to invent a character to go with the characters in item 1. For example

   - hairdresser/customer
   - secretary/boss.

4. You could ask them all to do a scene between the hairdresser and the customer, rehearse for five minutes and then perform the scene in front of the whole class. Remember that they must find the right voice for the character.

5. You may wish to let them choose for themselves from the above list, in which case allow them to rehearse for five minutes or so and then show the rest of the class what they have done. Again the voice is the most important thing and they must attempt an accent or a tone that will best express the character.

6. Ask them to choose one of the above characters and write a speech consisting of five or six sentences in which the character speaks to someone else. Each person must then speak their speech aloud and the class have to guess who the character is.

7. Get the class to write their own list of characters, either real or imaginary, and then ask each child to speak as that character. The class have to guess who the character is from the voice used.

8. Another way of doing it, as a game, is to ask each person to think of a character they would like to hear and then pick on someone in the class to speak a sentence as that character. For example

- I want you to speak as Kung Fu Panda
- I want you to speak as a head teacher
- I want you to speak as a judge
- I want you to speak as a character from *Eastenders*.

Variations

- Give points in item 8 to pupils on a scale of one to five. The winner is the person who has acquired the most points.

Melodrama (Voice Work)

This activity links up with the activities on pages 116 and 118. In this activity we focus on the vocal aspects of the style of acting known as Melodrama.

Suitable for

KS2

Cross-curriculum links

English, History

Aims

- To learn to overact.
- To project a broad characterisation.
- To experiment with vocal variation.

Resources

- An open space

What to do

1. Explain to the children that in Melodrama there is exaggeration in both movement and speech. Having already tackled movement in Part 1 we are now going to look at speech. Ask them, one at a time, to speak the following words and make a gesture to go with them. The class then repeats both the word and the gesture made. The more exaggerated, the better

   - Zounds!
   - Curses!
   - The devil!
   - I am undone!

- What's to be done?
- Unhand me, villain!
- You lie!
- Devil take you!
- You are my prisoner!
- Stop crying or I shall cut your throat!
- Stand still, you little devil!

2. Ask them to get into pairs as 'villain' and 'victim'. Ask them to speak the following lines and make exaggerated gestures to accompany the speech. Keep repeating until you are satisfied that they are overacting enough:

   (a) Villain: Get over here, you little devil!
       Victim: I will not, sir!
   (b) Villain: So, you defy me!
       Victim: Yes, I do. On my mother's life!
   (c) Villain: Do you see this knife?
       Victim: I fear no knives, nor you!
   (d) Villain: You will obey me!
       Victim: I would rather die first!
   (e) Villain: There is no one for miles around!
       Victim: I have faith in my God!

3. When they have rehearsed and got used to the above exchanges they can choose another person, making up a group of three, and rehearse the following speeches, making the appropriate gestures and using a suitable voice. They should remember what they learnt from Part 1 about exiting and raising the right hand, plus back of hand on forehead

   A: Who is this man, Matilda?
   B: He is to be my husband.
   A: Without my permission?
   B: I love him, father.
   C: She loves me, sir.
   A: You dog! You swine!
   B: Don't abuse him, father!
   C: Please, listen to me, sir!
   A: Get out of my house!
   B: Father, please!
   A: He must leave my house this instant!

C: I shall leave, sir, but I shall be back! (He exits.)

B: And I, father, shall go with him (She exits.)

A: And I shall stay here. Oh, woe is me!

4. Still in groups of three, they now work on the following Melodrama scenario and must remember to exaggerate. In other words it does not have to be realistic

Villain: I have you at last, my sweetling.

Victim: Release me, sir.

Villain: Why should I? I have you where I want you.

Victim: Have mercy, sir.

Hero (entering): Release her, sir, immediately!

Villain: Or else?

Hero: Or else I shall be forced to kill you!

Victim: Oh, do not fight on my account!

Hero & Villain (together): But we both love you!

Victim: Release me. I love neither of you.

Hero & Villain (together): What?!

Victim: I love another.

Hero & Villain: Who is it you love?

Victim: I love Godfrey!

Hero & Villain: Godfrey!

Victim: Yes, Godfrey.

Hero & Villain: But he is ...?

Victim: Yes, that's right.

Hero & Villain (at the same time): He is your brother!!

Victim: He is my brother!

Choral Speech

> In this activity we learn about 'speaking together' as a chorus. Choral speech is used in many plays.

Suitable for

KS1, KS2

Cross·curriculum link

English

Aims

- To improve timing.
- To learn to listen to others.
- To speak clearly.
- To project the voice.

Resources

- An open space

What to do

1. Speaking together, like singing together, is an important part of drama, as many plays for children are written with a strong contribution from a chorus. Ask the children to stand in a circle and select one person to be a main character. That person can go in the centre of the circle. The rest of the class are the chorus and must speak together. Try the following exchanges between a character and chorus

   King: Good morning, my subjects.
   Chorus: Good morning, Your Majesty.

   King: What should you say to me every morning?
   Chorus: Long live the King, Your Majesty.

King:	What should you do every morning?
Chorus:	Bow down and worship you, Your Majesty.
King:	Well, what are you waiting for?
Chorus:	We are waiting for your orders, Your Majesty.

Ask different children to play the part of the king (or queen if you like) until the chorus are used to timing its reply as precisely as possible.

Ask the chorus to add gestures and movement to its speech, for example bowing or curtsying.

2. Now try these exchanges in the same way with the class acting as chorus, or you can split the class into smaller groups

Sleeping Beauty (waking):	How long have I been asleep?
Chorus:	One hundred years, Your Highness.
Sleeping Beauty:	Can that be true?
Chorus:	Completely true.
Sleeping Beauty:	And what have you been doing?
Chorus:	We have been asleep too.
Sleeping Beauty:	Where are my father and mother?
Chorus:	They are still asleep, Your Highness.
Sleeping Beauty:	Where is Frederick, my Master of Ceremonies?
Chorus:	He is still asleep, Your Highness.
Sleeping Beauty:	Well, go and wake him. At once.
Chorus:	Yes, Your Majesty.
Sleeping Beauty:	And tell him to wake up my mother and father.
Chorus:	Yes, Your Majesty.

3. Ask the class to get into groups of five. One of them is to be a main character and the rest are the chorus and have to speak as one. They can choose from any story they know. For example

- Goldilocks and the three bears
- Cinderella
- Rumpelstiltskin.

Or they can create their own story with a chorus.

4. Ask them to get into groups of three and learn by heart the following lines from *Macbeth*

> When shall we three meet again
> In thunder, lightning or in rain?

It is the witches speaking and the children should all try to speak the lines as a chorus, adding movement and gesture to increase the effect.

Variations

- In items 1 and 2 the children can be asked to continue the scene. They can introduce new characters but the chorus has to remain.
- In item 3 they should be given time and help to either write down or discuss the development of the lines for character and chorus.

Mobile phones

Mobile phones have become a feature of modern life and most people, including young children, now possess one. There is much opportunity to create drama out of a mobile phone or a text message, and in this chapter we will investigate a few possibilities.

Suitable for

KS1, KS2

Cross-curriculum link

English

Aims

- To communicate through texting.
- To make a message clear to the person you phone.

Resources

- Paper and pencils

What to do

1. The children choose a partner with whom they want to work on having a mobile phone conversation about the following issues

   - you are a parent and phone the head teacher to say that your child has been bullied at school
   - you phone the police to report a noisy party going on next door
   - you are a parent and the head teacher phones you to say your child has been misbehaving.

   One partner phones up the other first and then they swap over. There is no need to use real mobiles for these activities.

2. Texting – ask each person in the class to write out a text message on a piece of paper and then fold the paper up and give it to someone in the class. You can choose who sends a text to whom or the children can choose. Each person then has to open the message and read it out loud to the rest of the class. Then that person has to write a reply. Each person has to read the message aloud and reply and so on.

3. As a pair work on the following ideas for a telephone conversation
   - you phone mum or dad from home to say that you have run out of bread, orange juice, tea and breakfast cereal
   - you are ill at home and phone up mum or dad at work to say that you can smell gas
   - you phone mum or dad from school to say that you are feeling sick and want to go home.

4. Write down a list of all the people you would like to phone if you had their telephone number and what you would like to ask them or say to them.

5. Write a text or telephone message to mum or dad saying
   - that you are feeling ill at school and are going home but have lost your key
   - you have eaten too much and have been sick
   - you have been bullied
   - you have won a prize
   - your team has won a sporting event at school.

The Travellers and the Bear (part 1)

A fable by Aesop

In this activity we are introduced to a fable by Aesop and find ways of examining the story from different points of view.

Suitable for

KS1, KS2

Cross-curriculum links

English, Art, History

Aims

- To identify sequences in a story.
- To write about a series of events.
- To select what is important in a dramatic sense.

Resources

- An open space

The Travellers and the Bear

Two friends were travelling on the same road together when they met with a bear.

One of them, in great fear and without thinking of the other, climbed up into a tree and hid himself.

The other, seeing that he had no chance, single handed against the bear, threw himself on the ground and pretended to be dead, for he had heard that a bear will never touch a dead body.

As he lay there, the bear came up to his head and smelt and sniffed him all over.

The man held his breath and the bear, supposing him to be dead, walked away.

When the bear was out of sight his friend came down out of the tree and asked what it was that the bear had whispered to him.

'I saw the bear put his mouth very close to your ear. What did he say to you?'

'It's no great secret', replied the other, 'the bear told me to take care of the company I keep, especially those who, when they get into difficulty, leave their friends in the lurch.'

What to do

1. Read the story to the children.

2. Explain what a fable is and discuss with them the moral of the story.

3. Draw a picture of any part of the story or recreate it using computer graphics.

4. Ask the class to choose one of the two friends from the story – either the one who climbed the tree or the other who lay on the ground – and write an account of what happened. For example, 'Yesterday I was walking through the woods with my friend Julian when a bear attacked us …'

5. Now ask them to write an account of what happened from the point of view of the other friend.

6. Next they should write an account from the point of view of the bear – and sign it with a paw mark!

7. Now ask the children to pretend to be a newspaper reporter, writing an article about the incident for their local paper.

8. Get them into pairs. One is a TV news reporter interviewing the two friends – separately – after the incident.

9. Next, the bear is talking to his mum and dad about what happened. Get the class into groups of three to improvise a conversation between the three bears. They can either use English or invent their own bear language.

The Travellers and the Bear (part 2)

In this activity we look at ways of using a dramatic speech approach to convey the drama of the story, still on the subject of Aesop's fables.

Suitable for

KS1 (optional), KS2

Cross-curriculum links

English, History

Aims

- To improve reading skills.
- To recognise punctuation marks.
- To learn how to vary the voice for dramatic effect.

Resources

- An open space

What to do

1. Get the class to sit in a circle and then give out a copy of the story to each person.
2. Ask each child to read a section of the story and stop at the first punctuation mark. The next person reads up to the next punctuation mark and so on until the end of the story.
3. Start them reading the story again, but this time with a different person starting so that everyone will have a different section to read.
4. Now get the class to stand up and read again up to punctuation marks, but this time ask them to put more expression and drama in their voices. Use some of the ideas already encountered in Melodrama.

5. Ask for three people to go into the centre of the circle. They are going to mime the actions as the circle reads the story. Give them time to do their mimes before moving on to the next section.

6. Now explain to the class that everyone will have a chance to be a fierce bear – if they wish. Read out the phrase 'they met with a bear'. Anyone in the circle – but only one at a time – can then go into the centre of the circle and be a fierce, growling bear. Tell them that the circle is protected by an invisible force so that the bear cannot touch anyone in the circle. Then try another person to be the bear, and so on. You could also try getting them to be

- King Kong
- Dracula
- a werewolf.

7. Get the class into groups of three. They are

- narrator
- bear
- person on the ground.

The narrator reads the sentence 'As he lay there, the bear came up to his head and smelt and sniffed him all over.' Then the bear does the action of sniffing while the body lies quite still. They can all have a go at being the bear.

8. In pairs, ask them to say the lines after the man comes down from the tree, but to say them in a whisper as if they are frightened the bear might still be around

- (in a whisper) 'I saw the bear put his mouth very close to your ear. What did he say to you?'
- (in a whisper) 'The bear told me to take care of the company I keep,'
- (even quieter) 'especially those who leave their friends in the lurch.'

Variations

- An interesting variation on item 6 is to suggest to the class that they are all scientists examining various animals in the centre of the circle. The scientists are protected by an invisible fence, so whoever goes into the centre as an animal cannot touch the scientists. The animals can move around the centre and go up to the scientists making growling noises but they cannot touch them.
- Another variation is to get the scientists to describe what they saw after an animal has been in the circle and give their analysis of what should be done with the animal.

The Ant and the Grasshopper

A fable by Aesop

> In this activity we examine another fable by Aesop and continue to find ways of dramatising the story through vocal techniques.

Suitable for

KS1, KS2

Cross-curriculum links

Art, English, History, PE

Aims

- To learn how to interpret a theme from a story.
- To experiment with vocal pitch and rhythm.

Resources

- An open space

The Ant and the Grasshopper

On a cold frosty day in winter an Ant was dragging out some of the corn which he had laid out in summertime, to dry it.

A Grasshopper, half-dead with hunger, begged the Ant to give him a morsel of it to preserve his life.

'What were you doing this last summer?', asked the Ant.

'Oh', said the Grasshopper. 'I was not idle. I was singing all the summer long.'

'Since you sang all summer, you can dance all winter', said the Ant, laughing, and shut up his granary.

What to do

1. Read the above story to the children, asking them to think about the meaning or moral of the story.

2. Look up Aesop in a book or on the internet and find out what other kind of stories he wrote.

3. In groups of three ask the children to read the story, with one of them as the narrator, the other as the Ant and the other as the Grasshopper.

4. Look at some pictures of ants and grasshoppers with the children and get them to do a simple drawing of each one.

5. Get them to spread out and discover ways of moving like an ant and a grasshopper.

6. Ask them to get into pairs. One is an ant, the other a grasshopper. Ask them to move in the following ways. The ant

   - slowly
   - deliberately
   - head looking round slowly
   - on knees and hands
   - working with effort.

   The grasshopper

   - leaping
   - looking around vacantly
   - bored
   - wasting time
   - crouching
   - dancing
   - jigging up and down.

7. Now ask the pairs to do what it says in the story. The ant lays out its corn to dry in the sun. The grasshopper hops round enjoying himself.

8. Now ask the pairs to think of a voice for the ant and the grasshopper. The ant could speak in a voice that is

   - slow
   - boring
   - monotonous
   - deep.

   The grasshopper could speak in a voice that is

   - high pitched
   - fast
   - singing.

9. The children could now get back into groups of three and read the story using the voices they have invented. The narrator should have a standard English voice.

The Hare and the Tortoise

A fable by Aesop

We look at more ways of experimenting with speech using another Aesop fable.

Suitable for

KS1, KS2

Cross-curriculum links

Art, PE

Aims

- To invent more accents.
- To learn to match voice with character.

The Hare and the Tortoise

A Hare was making fun of a Tortoise because of the slowness of his walk.

'I'll race you any day, if you like, but I bet I can beat you', said the Tortoise.

'All right', said the Hare, laughing. 'You shall soon see what my feet are made of.'

So it was agreed that they should start at once.

'I'll race you to that wall', said the Tortoise.

The Tortoise went off jogging along, without a moment's stopping, at his usual steady pace.

The Hare, treating the whole matter as a joke, said, 'I'll have a little nap first and overtake you later.'

Meanwhile the Tortoise plodded on.

The Hare smiled and, settling down under his favourite tree, fell into a deep sleep. She dreamt that she was the fastest creature on earth and winning every race imaginable. She was having some very pleasant dreams when she suddenly woke up and realised that she had overslept.

She saw the Tortoise in the distance and ran as fast as her legs could carry her, just in time to see the Tortoise touch the wall.

What to do

1. The class looks up pictures of hares and tortoises in books or on the internet. They may also find some film of them to see how these animals move.

2. Then the children could try drawing pictures of hares or tortoises and colouring them in.

3. Some energetic games at the beginning of the lesson should set things in motion for this story

   - Divide the class into two groups. One group are hares, the other are tortoises. On the command 'Hares!' the hare group must run as fast as they can across the room and back. On the command 'Tortoises' the tortoise group must go across the room and back in a slow, regular rhythm.

   - Now ask the hares and the tortoises to change roles and do the same thing again.

   - Ask them to find a partner. One of them is a hare, the other is a tortoise. Each pair has a go with the rest of the class watching. On your command the hare must race across the room as many times as possible while the tortoise simply does one crossing, slowly. When the tortoise reaches the other end of the room everything stops and you calculate how many crossings the hare has made. The watching class can count aloud how many times the hare has crossed the room.

   - When every pair has had a go, ask them to change roles so that everyone can feel what it's like to be a hare and a tortoise.

4. Now we are going to concentrate on the kind of voices that the hare and the tortoise have. Ask the whole class to speak the following line all together very slowly and in a deep voice

   - I'll race you any day, if you like, but I bet I can beat you.

   Now go round the class and ask each person to say the line on their own. Then ask the whole class to speak the following line as quickly and excitedly as possible

   - All right, you shall soon see what my feet are made of.

   Now go round the class and ask each person to say the line on their own.

5. Divide the class into two groups, a hare group and a tortoise group. Ask the tortoises to say the following line together

- I'll race you to that wall.

Now ask the hare group to say the following line all together

- I'll have a little nap first and overtake you later.

6. Keep the class divided into the two large groups and make them stand at opposite ends of the room. They must speak the lines of the hare and the tortoise, all speaking together as a chorus

Tortoises:	I'll race you any day, if you like, but I bet I can beat you.
Hares:	All right, you shall soon see what my feet are made of.
Tortoises:	I'll race you to that wall.
Hares:	I'll have a little nap first and overtake you later.

7. Now get them into pairs again. One is the hare and the other is the tortoise. They practise saying the above lines in the right character voice for the hare and the tortoise. Each pair can perform in front of the rest of the class to see who has the best character voice.

8. *The Hare's Dream* – ask the children to pretend to fall asleep then act out the following

- wake up, but you are dreaming
- you strut around as if you are an Olympic champion at the end of a race that you have won
- you hear the applause of the crowd
- you receive the winner's cup and a medal
- you do a lap of honour waving to the crowd, who are all cheering you
- you sink to the ground slowly and fall asleep again
- you suddenly wake up and realise that the tortoise is far ahead of you.

9. Now you ask each pair to prepare a little scenario based on the story, including both movement and speech.

Variations

- In item 8 you could either get the children to act out the sequence together or one at a time with the rest of the class watching.
- In item 9 the children can invent their own additional dialogue if they wish.

The Fox and the Crow

A fable by Aesop

In this activity we read and enact another of Aesop's famous fables.

Suitable for

KS1, KS2

Cross-curriculum links

English, History, Art

Aims

- To add more vocal variations.

Resources

- Recordings of bird sounds

The Fox and the Crow

A Crow had snatched a large piece of cheese out of a window and flew with it high into a tree to enjoy his prize.

A Fox spied the delicious piece of cheese and determined to have it.

'O Crow', said the Fox. 'What beautiful wings you have, what lovely bright eyes you have and how graceful is your pretty neck. It's such a shame that you can't sing otherwise you'd be the cleverest bird on earth.'

The Crow, flattered by the Fox's fine words, thought he would surprise the Fox with his fine voice. He opened his mouth and down the cheese dropped, straight into the Fox's mouth.

After the Fox had chewed and swallowed the delicious piece of cheese he said to the Crow, 'I really meant what I said about your beauty, but I hadn't yet said anything about your brains.'

What to do

1. Ask the class to close their eyes and imagine they are munching the following
   - their favourite crisps
   - their favourite sweet
   - their favourite jam
   - a boiled egg
   - a fried egg
   - a piece of juicy bacon
   - baked beans
   - chips
   - a beefburger
   - a cheeseburger.

2. Now ask them one by one to mime eating their favourite food and the rest of the class have to guess what they are eating.

3. Now ask them to be a crow
   - perched on a branch high up in a tree
   - they see their favourite food down below in an open kitchen window
   - they swoop down and take it
   - they fly back up to their branch to enjoy it.

4. If possible have some recordings of bird sounds. Play them the sound a crow makes – a caw. Get them into groups of four or five and ask them to practise flying and cawing together. Have a competition for the best group of crows by performing in front of the class.

5. Ask them to get into pairs as two crows. They are cold and hungry. It is the middle of winter. They have not eaten for two days. Ask them to improvise a conversation about this, paying particular attention to the kind of voice a crow has.

6. Suddenly they see a piece of cheese in a window down below. They must describe what they see. What do they do?

7. Now ask the class to focus on the fox. Ask them to creep around the room as quietly as possible, looking around for food. The key words are
   - silent movement
   - sniffing
   - creeping
   - watching
   - listening.

8. Ask them to get into pairs. One is fox and the other is crow. Ask them to repeat the following type of conversation in order to practise the 'voice' and 'accent' they are to adopt in order to make a vocal contrast

   Fox: Good morning, Mrs Crow.
   Crow: Good morning, Mr Fox.

Fox: How are you today, Mrs Crow?
Crow: Very well, thank you, Mr Fox.

Fox: You're looking very nice today, Mrs Crow.
Crow: Thank you, Mr Fox.

Fox: In fact you're looking beautiful, Mrs Crow.
Crow: That's very flattering, Mr Fox. Thank you.

Fox: In fact I've never seen you looking so beautiful.
Crow: That's very kind of you, Mr Fox.

Fox: Your wings are so pretty.
Crow: Thank you.

Fox: Your eyes are so bright.
Crow: Thank you.

Fox: The varnish on your claws is such a divine colour.
Crow: Oh, Mr Fox, you are such a gentleman.

The fox should speak in a voice that is

- oily
- flattering
- masculine.

The crow should speak in a voice that is

- feminine
- simpering
- flustered.

9. When they have adopted a voice ask them to make up their own conversation in which the fox flatters the crow.

10. Now they can practise in their pairs the story as outlined in the Aesop fable. They can show the class what they have done at the end of the lesson when they have had sufficient rehearsal.

Variations

- The lesson could start with the children drawing the crow and the fox.
- Look up on the internet the habits of foxes and crows and make a list of the food they like to eat.

Pronouncing Difficult Words

In this activity we look at ways of pronouncing long or difficult words and attempt some 'tongue twisters'.

Suitable for

KS1, KS2

Cross-curriculum links

English, Art

Aims

- To show vocal clarity.
- To show vocal projection.

What to do

1. The class can either be seated at their desks or sitting on the floor in a circle if there is sufficient space. Ask them to do the following
   - open mouths wide
   - say 'Aaahhh'
   - open mouths small
   - say 'Aaaahh'
   - grit teeth
   - say 'Aaaahh'.

   Practise this a number of times in the following ways
   - loudly
   - quietly
   - eagerly
   - sadly.

2. Now ask the class to repeat together the following
   - How, now, brown cow.
   - The rain in Spain stays mainly in the plain.
   - Double, double toil and trouble.
   - Fire burn and cauldron bubble.

Practise these a number of times in the following ways

- opening the mouth very big
- opening the mouth very wide
- opening the mouth very small
- slowly and deliberately
- as fast as possible but not gabbling.

3. If possible find the poem called 'Romance' by A.J. Turner. Read it through with the children and concentrate on pronouncing the following difficult words, which are all volcanoes in South America

- Chimborazo
- Popacatapetle.
- Cotopaxi

Split the names into syllables and pronounce them separately until the whole word can be pronounced with confidence either by the whole class or individually.

There are some nice images in this poem that can be used as the basis for a colourful picture or a drawing.

4. There is a poem by Charles Causley called 'Colonel Fazakerley' that can be read by the class. The main character has a rather long, pompous name

- Colonel Fazakerley Butterworth-Toast.

Ask the children to try to pronounce this name and to try to picture the Colonel. Perhaps a drawing here would be appropriate.

Ask the children to make up their own long-winded names. Here are some examples

- Mr and Mrs Throat-Warbler-Mangrove
- Lord and Lady Ponsonby-Ploop
- The Duchess of Loxely-Langrove
- The Duke of Finistry-Bloggs-Haven.

5. Tongue twisters are very useful to get children to think about speaking clearly and precisely. Here are a few they can practise either individually, in pairs or as a whole class

- she sells sea shells on the sea shore
- old, oily, Ollie
- Peter Piper picked a peck of pickled peppers
- red lorry, yellow lorry
- three free throws.

Soundscapes

In this activity we learn how to create atmosphere by the use of sounds and words.

Suitable for

KS1, KS2

Cross-curriculum link

English

Aims

- To demonstrate careful listening.
- To show awareness of vocal potential for creating atmosphere.

Resources

- An open space

What to do

1. Ask the children to create an eerie night-time soundscape, using the following idea

   - a whistling wind.

   When this has been established ask one or two children to add the following

   - an owl hooting
   - a crow cawing.

   Now add the following sounds from various children

   - a ghostly sound
   - a tree creaking in the wind.

   Now ask several to add the sound of

- a horse trotting along
- someone knocking on a door
- a dog barking.

Once roles have been allotted to the children ask them all to close their eyes and start from the beginning with the wind. Then they add any other sounds that are appropriate. They should keep their eyes firmly shut and listen carefully.

2. There is a poem called 'The Listeners' by Walter de la Mare that could be read as an example of mood painting with words. Here are a few ideas that could be used together with the above soundscape

- a horseman approaches
- he gets off his horse
- he approaches the door of an old building
- he knocks on the door
- he asks if there's anybody there
- there is no answer
- he calls again
- there is no answer
- is there somebody in the building watching and listening?
- the horseman gets on his horse
- he rides off.

3. Here is another scenario, called 'Dracula's Castle', that can be used with a soundscape. Children can be used either as characters or soundscape or both. Dialogue can be added by the children

- a four-horse stagecoach is heard travelling along a country road
- there is wind, thunder and lightning
- the coach crashes into a rock and a wheel breaks off
- the occupants of the coach are a wealthy family
- they are stuck in the middle of nowhere
- they see a light in the distance
- they approach an old, sinister castle
- they knock on the door
- an old servant opens the door
- they may stay the night
- the master comes down and welcomes them
- they are brought drinks
- they fall asleep.

4. The children can decide what happens next by writing a story or a play to continue the above.

5. Another good soundscape idea is called 'Farmyard Waking Up'. In this the atmosphere of morning can be created by the use of sound. Get the children to sit in a circle with their eyes shut and ask them to make the following sounds.

- birds
- cuckoos
- dogs barking
- frogs
- ducks
- pigs
- hens.

It is important they keep their eyes shut when listening.

The Splendour Falls on Castle Walls

A poem by Alfred Lord Tennyson

In this activity we study a poem called 'The Splendour Falls On Castle Walls' by Alfred Lord Tennyson, and employ drama techniques of choral and individual speech to convey the poem's meaning.

Suitable for

KS2

Cross-curricular links

English, Art, History

Aims

- To become aware of the power of words in recitation.
- To speak together.
- To show awareness of rhythm in poetry.

Resources

- Recording of a bugle
- *Lord of the Rings* music

The Splendour Falls on Castle Walls

The splendour falls on castle walls
And snowy summits old in story:
The long light shakes across the lakes
And the wild cataract leaps in glory.
Blow, bugle, blow, set the wild echoes flying,
Blow, bugle; answer, echoes, dying, dying, dying.

O hark, O hear! How thin and clear,
And thinner, clearer, farther going!

O sweet and far from cliff and scar
The horns of Elfland faintly blowing!
Blow, let us hear the purple glens replying:
Blow, bugle; answer, echoes, dying, dying, dying.

What to do

1. First of all the children should know something about Alfred Lord Tennyson, so either give them some information or let them research him in their ICT lesson.

2. Read the poem through with the children and ask them to tell you what images and pictures they can see in the poem. Their answers may be one or all of the following

   - castle walls
   - snowy summits
   - light across the lakes
   - waterfall
   - a bugle
   - cliffs and rocks
   - purple glens.

3. Ask them to draw a picture of their favourite image from the poem or create a computer graphics image.

4. Ask the children what they understand by the word 'Elfland'.

5. Ask them what sounds they can hear from the poem. You may have answers such as

   - waterfall
   - sound of a bugle
   - echoes from across the lake
   - the horns of Elfland.

6. Ask the children if they think there is a story in this poem. Ask them what the meaning of the poem is for them.

7. Ask them to write down all the words that rhyme

   - falls – walls
   - shakes – lakes, etc.

8. Using groups of children to speak various lines you could suggest the following, but this will depend on the number of children in your class

Line 1: A group of four

Line 2: Another group of four

Line 3: Another group of four

Line 4: Another group of four

Line 5: Everyone says 'Blow, bugle, blow'

Line 5: Line 1 people say 'set the wild echoes flying'

Line 6: Everyone says 'Blow, bugle; answer, echoes'

Line 6: Line 2 people say 'dying'

Line 3 people say 'dying' (quietly)

Line 4 people say 'dying' (very quietly).

9. You could use smaller groups to recite the whole poem, using the above pattern. Groups of six should be sufficient.

Variations

- A recording of a bugle would be helpful to set the atmosphere for the poem.
- Sections of music from *Lord of the Rings* would also be suitable to play to the children as an aid to atmosphere.
- A competition could be organised at the end of the lesson for both the group that can recite the poem by heart and the clearest speakers.

Improvisation Starters (Family Life)

In this activity we look at various starting points for spoken improvisations which can be developed into more polished work.

Suitable for

KS2

Cross-curriculum link

English

Aims

- To show awareness of how accents can reveal character in drama.
- To learn to think quickly.
- To play different age groups.

What to do

1. Explain to the class that you are going to give them starting points for spoken improvisations concerning family life. They are to be divided into groups of four. All the roles are young people of their own age speaking to each other. You give them a starting line and one minute to prepare a scene

   - I wish my family were different
   - I wish my family had more exciting holidays
   - I wish my family had more money
   - I wish my family had greater interest in me
   - I wish my family took me out more often.

   After initial preparation each group can perform in front of the others if they wish to.

   Further development can take place for those groups who wish to polish any of their improvisations further. They can have more time for rehearsal and preparation, using props and costumes if they wish.

2. In groups of four to six people they are now going to work on building up scenes for an overall title. The title is 'A Day at the Beach'.

The roles are various members of the family

- mum
- dad
- grandma or grandad
- two children (of own age).

Once they have allotted roles tell them that the scenes are as follows

- at home – planning when and where to go
- in the car – the journey itself
- at the beach – what happens there.

Suggest that there should be a narrator who is the person who tells the story in flashback. Here is a suggested starter for the narrator

Narrator

It all started last Friday when I came home from school. Mum told me that dad had had this wonderful idea of having a day at the beach on Sunday. Oh, by the way, my name is Gary and that's my mum over there cooking in the kitchen. Dad isn't home from work yet. He usually gets in about 6 o'clock and tells us about what a boring day he's had at work. That's gran sitting in the chair watching telly. She's half blind and can't really see the telly and she's deaf as well which means she has to guess what they're saying half the time. Anyhow that's how the weekend started ...

3. When working on improvisations involving family life it is sometimes fun to put all the dads together to have a moan at some point in the rehearsal process. You could also do the same with the grannies, the mums and the children. It provides another perspective on the characters and can lead to a lot of funny scenes. The locations could be as follows

- dads – meet at the local pub
- grans – meet at the old folks centre
- mums – meet at a coffee morning
- kids – meet at school.

4. In the same groups, or they can change now, ask them to develop a spoken improvisation based on two totally opposite types of family. One is called

- the Highbrows.

And the other is called

- the Lowbrows.

The Highbrows are

- clever
- caring
- articulate
- book readers
- readers of quality newspapers

- well dressed
- well off
- frequent holiday makers
- used to eating out
- home owners.

The Lowbrows are

- stupid
- selfish
- poorly educated
- badly dressed

- not at all well off
- a 'days at the beach' family
- fish and chip eaters
- living in a disgusting home.

Divide the class into 'The Highbrows' and 'The Lowbrows'. As an additional idea each family group can start their scene speaking as a chorus with the following suggested lines:

Highbrows: We are the Highbrows and we live in a house.
Lowbrows: We are the Lowbrows and we live in a slum.

Highbrows: We the Highbrows and we holiday in the Bahamas.
Lowbrows: We are the Lowbrows and we holiday in Bognor.

Highbrows: We are the Highbrows and we read *The Times*.
Lowbrows: We are the Lowbrows and we can't read.

Highbrows: We are the Highbrows and we drive a BMW.
Lowbrows: We are the Lowbrows and we drive an old van.

5. Another idea for this kind of 'social' improvisation is to put two Highbrow groups together, speaking about a Lowbrow family. The conversation can centre on the following subjects

- the Lowbrows' house
- their garden
- their van
- the way they dress
- the things they eat
- their personal hygiene.

6. Two Lowbrow families can be put together to converse about a Highbrow family. Subjects for conversation could include

- the Highbrows' new car(s)
- their house
- their posh friends
- the fact that they never speak to the Lowbrows.

Spoken Improvisation Work

> In this activity we deal with ways in which children can develop logical sequences into spoken improvisations.

Suitable for

KS2

Cross-curriculum link

English

Aims

- To thinking logically.
- To show awareness of nouns.
- To show awareness of verbs.

Resources

- An open space
- Pen and paper

What to do

1. Ask the class to write down on a piece of paper or in their English books a logical sequence of actions they perform. It could be

   - I get up at 7.30 every day
   - then I have a wash

   or

   - on Saturdays I get up at 8 o'clock
   - then I usually go swimming with my friend

   or

   - on Sundays I get up at 9 o'clock
   - then I play on my computer.

After they have written a series of at least ten actions ask some of them to read theirs out.

2. Ask the class to either sit at their desks or in a circle. Explain that they are going to talk about actions they perform every day. They must each contribute a logical progression from the person before them. For example, one person starts by saying

- every day I get up at 7.30.

The next person might say

- then I have a wash.

The next person might say

- then I get dressed.

You progress round the circle, each person describing an action or describing an event that could logically happen in sequence. Encourage them to be as detailed as possible. For example

- I have a wash but it's often so cold in the bathroom I don't stay in there for long.
- I try to get into the bathroom but my sister usually gets in first so I have to wait ages.
- I get dressed in my boring school uniform.

3. Now ask the children to start with a time of day, and each person has to say a time and describe what happens at that time. The next person goes to the next time of day in which something happens, and so on. For example

- 1st person: at 7.30 I get up
- 2nd person: at 7.32 I have a wash
- 3rd person: at 7.35 I get dressed
- 4th person: at 7.45 I go down to breakfast
- 5th person: At 7.46 my mum puts breakfast on the table.

4. Ask them now to build up a picture of what happens in the course of a typical school day. They can write about it first and then read it out.

5. In the circle ask them to each describe a series of events that happened to them that day, from the moment they woke up. Remind them that they must try to describe each action in logical sequence, without missing anything out, and be as detailed as possible.

6. Explain that you are now going to require them to do some mime actions with their spoken descriptions. This time they are not allowed to speak any verbs, they have to mime the action that the verb describes. For example

- I (clean) my teeth, (wash) my face and (go) downstairs.

Instead of saying all of the above they must mime the actions in brackets.

Here are some more examples to give them if they cannot think of any themselves

- I (leave) the house at about 8.45, (walk) to the nearest bus stop and (get on) the bus when it (comes along).
- I (enter) school at 9 o'clock, (run) to my classroom, (take out) my books from my satchel and (sit down) to write.
- When the teacher (comes in), we all (stand up) and (throw) banana skins at him.

7. The same kind of exercise can be done eliminating the nouns. You have to mime all nouns. For example

- My (mum) shouts at me because I am always late for (breakfast) and my little (sister) laughs.
- In the (morning) I usually have (eggs), (bacon) and (tomatoes) as well as baked (beans) and (potatoes).

8. Put the class into pairs and ask them to prepare a spoken improvisation in which they have to describe a series of logical actions or events. Here are some starting lines to get them going

- What did you do this morning before you came to school?
- What lessons do you have in the morning?
- What do you do when school finishes?
- What do you do in the evenings?
- What do you do on Saturday mornings?
- What do you do on Sunday evening?

Variations

- In the miming verbs and nouns items the children might find it easier if they write down their sentences first before attempting to act them out.

A Day at the Beach

We focus in this activity on family groups and explore what happens when a family has a day out at the seaside.

Suitable for

KS1

Cross-curriculum link

English

Aims

- To work together as a group.
- To learn how to negotiate with others.

Resources

- An open space
- Some simple props such as sunglasses, various hats, scarves and beachwear

What to do

1. Get into groups of four or five. Each group is a family that is going to have a day out at the beach, but first they need to decide who their characters are going to be. They can choose from the following

   - mum
   - dad
   - grandma
   - grandad
   - a favourite friend
   - son or daughter
   - a teacher

When they have decided on characters discuss how the family is going to get to the beach

- by car
- rail
- bus
- walking.

Then discuss what they are going to take with them

- buckets and spades
- swimwear
- sunglasses
- sandals
- coats (if it rains)
- hats
- games.

Plan the first scene together and consider one of the following reasons

- mum or dad announce that you are going to the beach to celebrate your birthday
- it is a school trip so there will be a few teachers
- you have won a competition and the prize is a day out at the beach
- you and your best friend want to go and ask your parents if you can have a day out at the beach.

2. The second scene is the journey. Ask the children to discuss ideas in their groups and act out a few trial scenes ensuring that everybody in the group has an equal amount of participation.

3. The third scene is at the seaside. Ask the children to discuss some of the following ideas before they start acting the scene

- you are hungry when you get there
- it is too hot
- it starts to rain
- one of you gets lost
- one of you has an accident
- one of your party has a phone call to say your Uncle Bill is in hospital
- you see a big shark.

4. You can skip the return journey if you like and go straight back to your house or wherever you started from. Ask the children to discuss the following suggestions for the last scene

- you have your tea and talk about what has happened
- talk about whether you'd go to the beach again
- talk about where you would like to go next on an outing.

5. Finally each group can present their little play about the beach as a continuous performance in front of the rest of the class.

Variations

Suitable sound effects can be used at different stages in the play like

- the lapping of waves
- the sound of an ice-cream van
- a car starting up and driving off
- pop music.

Character Box Conversations

> In this activity we develop spoken improvisations from a list of words in the 'character box'.

Suitable for

KS2

Cross-curriculum link

English

Aims

- To create instant character types.
- To vocalise character types.
- To show movement of character types.

Resources

- Exercise books
- Thin white card
- A small box

What to do

1. Ask the children to write down in their English exercise books or on a piece of paper as many jobs and professions as they can think of. You may help them with the spelling of difficult words such as 'architect' or 'psychiatrist'. Typical examples of what they might come up with are 'plumber', 'teacher', 'footballer', 'detective', 'magician', 'chimney sweep'.

2. Write down on the board all the suggestions that the children have made.

3. Get some pieces of thin white card and cut them up into small strips. Write down or get the children to write down the names of as many

jobs and professions as possible. Put all the pieces of card into a 'character box'. This box then becomes the focal centre of many drama lessons and can be used either for movement work (see Part 1) or vocal work.

4. Get the class into pairs. Pass the box round the class. Each pair picks one card from the box. One of them must be the character on the card and the other person is an 'interviewer'. Each group prepares an interview improvisation in which the interviewer will ask questions of the character on the card. The children can decide for themselves on the type of interview – radio, television, as part of the news, an arts programme, a documentary, a magazine or newspaper interview.

5. Now get them into groups of three. One of them is the interviewer and the other two are from the world of sport. You can choose from any sport with which you are familiar

• football	• ice hockey
• swimming	• baseball
• rugby	• horse racing
• athletics	• snooker
• cricket	• darts
• tennis	• gymnastics
• basketball	• ice skating.

Or any other sport the children can think of.

Variations

- In item 1 they can complete this as part of an ICT lesson by looking up lists of professions.
- For item 4 they can change roles or choose a new character from the box.
- In item 5 you could, of course, create a sports box in which there are only names of well-known sports and let the children pick one from the box.

Loopy Dialogues (part 1)

This activity deals with funny 'loop dialogues' in which children are given a very short piece of conversation that they must learn by heart and repeat.

Suitable for

KS1 (optional), KS2

Cross-curriculum link

English

Aims

- To learn to focus on repeated actions.
- To learn not to laugh.

What to do

1. Explain to the children that a loop dialogue is a piece of speech for two or three characters that must be learnt by heart and repeated in exactly the same way a second time and a third time and a fourth time until a mistake is made or the children cannot continue because of laughter.

Go Away

Person 1 (opening a door): Oh, it's you.
Person 2: Yes, it's me.

Person 1: What do you want?
Person 2: To see you.

Person 1: Go away! (Slams door.)

2. Here is another short extract for two people.

Come In

Person 1 (opening door): Well, hello.
Person 2: Were you expecting me?

Person 1: Yes, I was.
Person 2: Shall I come in?

Person 1: Yes, of course. (Person 2 goes in and Person 1 closes the door.)

3. Again a short extract for two.

Did You See That?

Person 1 (pointing at the sky): Did you see that?
Person 2: No, what was it?

Person 1: It was a spaceship.
Person 2: Are you sure?

Person 1: I'm positive
Person 2: You're mad!

4. And another one for two people.

Where's Your Homework?

Teacher (pointing to pupil): What's your name?
Pupil: Henry Higgins.

Teacher: Have you done your homework?
Pupil: Yes.

Teacher: Well, where is it?
Pupil: It's at home.

Teacher (furious): What's it doing there?
Pupil: I forgot to bring it in.

5. A family extract for three people.

Family Scene

Mum: Sit down and eat your breakfast.
Child: Don't want it.

Dad: Eat it, it's good for you.
Child: Don't want it!
Dad: Sit down!
Mum (to Dad): Don't shout, dear.
Dad: I said, sit down!
Mum: Do what your father tells you.
Child: He hates me.
Mum: So do I!
Child: I'm going (Goes out.)

Loopy Dialogues (part 2)

This activity continues the idea of repeating scenes exactly and precisely.

Suitable for

KS1 (optional), KS2

Cross-curriculum link

English

Aims

- To show vocal precision.
- To remember lines.
- To improve timing.
- To create character from names.
- To interpret character from dialogue.

What to do

1. Get the class into pairs to repeat the following exactly.

Restaurant

Mr Loopy: Waiter! Waiter!
Waiter (running over): Yes, sir.

Mr Loopy: There's a fly in my soup!
Waiter (looking): I can't see it, sir.

Mr Loopy: Well, you must be blind.
Waiter (picking up the soup): I'll get you another, sir. (Walks off.)

Hairdresser

Mrs Loopy (sitting under the dryer): Mandy! Mandy! My hair's on fire!
Mandy (grabbing a fire extinguisher): I'll put it out, Mrs Loopy.

Mrs Loopy: Don't you dare aim that thing at me!
Mandy: Well, what am I to do?

Mrs Loopy: Ring the Fire Brigade!
Mandy: But you'll be dead by then.

Mrs Loopy: That can't be helped.
Mandy: I'll be sacked for this.

2. Get the class into groups of three and ask them to repeat the following dialogue

At the Bus Stop

(Mr and Mrs Loopy are waiting for a bus. Enter naughty schoolgirl, Shirl, chewing gum. They look at her.)

Shirl: What you looking at?
Mrs Loopy: I beg your pardon?

Shirl: I said, what you looking at?
Mr Loopy: Don't you be so cheeky.

Shirl: Shut up, grandad.
Mrs Loopy: Well, I never!

Mr Loopy: Young people, nowadays!
Mrs Loopy: No manners at all!

Mr Loopy: I'll report you to your school.
Shirl: Something smells at this bus stop.

Mr Loopy: Well, I assure you it's not me.
Shirl (looking at Mrs Loopy): No, it's probably her.
Mrs Loopy: Insufferable girl!

Stating Intentions

In this activity the children state what they are going to say or do and then do it.

Suitable for

KS1 (optional), KS2

Cross-curriculum link

English

Aims

- To write down what you intend to say.
- To speak your thoughts.
- To improvise with a partner from a given starting point.

What to do

1. Ask the children to stand in a circle and state what they are going to do, then they must do it. For example one person starts off by saying
   - I'm going to sit down because I'm tired.

   And then he/she does it. The next person can say
   - I'm going to remain standing and fold my arms.

   And then he/she does it.

   Go round the circle until everyone has had a turn.

2. Ask them to think about a series of two actions, then write them down.

3. They must now memorise their actions and perform them in front of the class. The class have to guess exactly what was written on the paper.

4. Ask them to think of a series of three actions and write them down.

5. They must now memorise their actions and perform them in front of the class.

6. Now ask the children to write down what they intend to say to someone. For example

- I'm going to tell mum that I don't want to go to school today because I'm feeling unwell.

Or

- I'm going to tell my friend that I don't like her new dog.

7. Ask them to write down the actual speech.

8. Now they choose someone from the class to be either 'mum' or 'the friend' and read the speech to them.

9. They should now both continue the situation as a piece of spoken dialogue and improvise a scene from that starting point, seeing how much they can both say to each other.

The Crowd – Mrs Pankhurst

It has been said that when you are part of a crowd you lose your identity. In this session we are going to use drama to be different kinds of crowds and also look at a famous character from history.

Suitable for

KS2

Cross-curriculum links

English, History

Aims

- To work together as a large group.
- To work together as a small group.
- To learn to research for information.

Resources

- An open space
- Use of the internet

What to do

1. Call out various types of crowd or locations and ask the pupils to blend together to form a whole bunch of people

   - a crowd waiting for a pop singer to arrive
   - a crowd waiting for a train which is late
   - a crowd watching a tennis match
   - a crowd watching a football match
   - a crowd cheering a 100-metres athletics race
   - an audience watching a horror film at a cinema

- a crowd watching a cat being rescued from a tree
- a crowd celebrating the New Year chimes of Big Ben.

Before starting work on these you can arrange the class to form different patterns for the different events.

2. Select one person to be the focus of the crowd's attention in the following scenarios

- a famous actor being surrounded by people wanting his autograph
- the Prime Minister being surrounded by protestors
- a religious leader being worshipped by a crowd
- a thief being chased by a crowd
- a flying saucer landing and an alien getting out.

3. As a break from the fun of the drama class ask the children to go to their desks and do some research into the life and times of Emmeline Pankhurst (1858–1928), a British political activist and leader of the British suffragette movement, which helped women win the right to vote. After a brief history lesson on Mrs Pankhurst you can go back to the drama class.

4. Ask the children to get into groups of about six. Each group forms a small part of a bigger crowd. Tell them that they are part of a crowd watching Mrs Pankhurst talking about votes for women in the year 1913. The group can have a discussion about the right to vote taking different sides

- two people agree that women should have the right to vote
- two people completely disagree
- two people can see both sides of the argument.

5. Let all the groups join together now and ask them to react as a crowd to what Mrs Pankhurst is saying.

Here is a short speech by Mrs Pankhurst, which can be read out by a member of the class while the crowd are reacting to her words.

'Put them in prison', they said, 'that will stop it.' But it didn't stop it at all: instead of the women giving it up, more women did it, and more and more and more women did it until there were 300 women at a time, who had not broken a single law, only 'made a nuisance of themselves' as the politicians say.

Now, I want to say to you who think women cannot succeed, we have brought the government of England to this position, that it has to face this alternative: either women are to be killed or women are to have the vote. I ask American men in this meeting, what would you say if in your state you were faced with that alternative, that you must either kill them or give them their citizenship? Well, there is only one answer to that alternative, there is only one way out – you must give those women the vote.

The children can react in the following ways

- calling out in agreement
- cheering
- shouting aggressively
- booing
- waving arms
- pointing
- hissing
- clapping
- stamping feet
- pushing others
- chanting slogans
- being unpleasant to others in the crowd
- shouting in support
- being fanatical.

6. As a final session, or perhaps on another day, the class could have a discussion chaired by the teacher in which the topics would be

- the right to express your opinion in public
- freedom of expression
- should there be censorship?
- what are privacy laws?
- should there be freedom of the press?
- what are human rights?

Dramatic Pause

> In this activity we study how a pause during or after speech can be just as effective as speech itself.

Suitable for

KS2

Cross-curriculum link

English

Aims

- To improve timing.
- To work as a chorus.

Resources

- DVD of *Goodbye, Mr Chips* with Robert Donat

What to do

1. Get the class into groups of four or five. Give each group a number. If there are five groups then tell them that Group 1 is the quietest speaking group and Group 5 is the loudest speaking group. Each group must say the following words in chorus followed by silence, starting with Group 1 in a whisper, then Group 2 quietly, then Group 3 louder, etc. They all attempt the same word before moving on to the next one. At the end of each round of words ask them which group had the best dramatic pause

   - No.
   - It can't be.
   - Are you sure?
   - God!
   - Finish it!
   - Yes.

2. Each group should now say a line as a chorus, followed by silence, followed by the next part of the line. The lines are

- No! Don't do it! … (silence) … I told you.
- Please, tell me! … (silence) … is it serious?
- Are you mad? … (silence) … it's not possible.
- They're coming … (silence) … didn't I tell you?
- Can you hear it? … (silence) … can you hear it?
- Oh, my God, just listen to that … (silence) … that's amazing.
- Teacher's coming … (silence) … it's all right, she's gone past.

Discuss with the class which group had the most effective dramatic pause and why.

3. Another very effective way of obtaining a dramatic pause is if there is a lot of noise and suddenly silence because somebody has come into the room. Divide the class into two halves for this and give them the following ideas to play around with

- A class of pupils is being really noisy and naughty when a head teacher walks in.

You may wish to show them an extract from the film *Goodbye, Mr Chips* where there is a good example of this towards the beginning

- Another scenario could be a class singing a rude song about a strict teacher when, lo and behold, the teacher walks in!

Variations

- In items 1 and 2 you can change the groups around from loudest to quietest. In fact it would be better to give them all a go at being loudest and quietest.

The Owl and the Pussycat (part 1)

A poem by Edward Lear

> In this activity we work on drama ideas for a part of Edward Lear's famous poem 'The Owl and the Pussycat'.

Suitable for

KS1, KS2

Cross-curriculum links

Art, English, History

Aims

- To achieve precision in choral speech.
- To show clear articulation.
- To create character voices.

Resources

- Photocopies of the poem

The Owl and the Pussycat (part 1)

The Owl and the Pussycat went to sea
In a beautiful pea green boat,
They took some honey, and plenty of money,
Wrapped up in a five pound note.
The Owl looked up to the stars above,
And sang to a small guitar,
'O lovely Pussy! O Pussy my love,
What a beautiful pussy you are,
You are,
You are!
What a beautiful pussy you are!'
Pussy said to the Owl, 'You elegant fowl!

How charmingly sweet you sing!
O let us be married! Too long we have tarried:
But what shall we do a for a ring?'

What to do

1. Ask the children to work in pairs. One is the owl, the other is the cat.
They must recite the poem to each other in the following way

- every reference to the owl must be spoken by the owl
- every reference to the pussycat must be spoken by the pussycat
- every reference to them both must be spoken by both of them
  in chorus.

2. After the initial recitation ask them to think about a particular type of
voice for the two animals. Ask them to make the voices as contrasted
as possible. They could consider any or all of the following

- (for the owl) deep throated, very masculine, smooth, silky
- (for the cat) feminine, musical, breathy, timid.

Now ask them to recite their 'speeches' to each other, for example

The Owl: O lovely Pussy! O Pussy my love (etc.)

Pussy: You elegant fowl! (etc.)

3. To add 'character' to the speeches ask them to use any of the following
suggested movements and gestures to go with the recitation

- (the owl) hand on heart, strumming a guitar, on one knee, looking
  up adoringly, extravagant gestures
- (the cat) hands clasped together, sitting elegantly with legs crossed,
  hand to cheek, back of hand to forehead.

4. Now ask them to recite their speeches to each other, using

- their new-found voices
- posture or movement
- hand and/or facial gestures.

5. After working on the above aspects they should be asked to recite the
whole poem using everything they have learnt so far. Each pair could
'perform' in front of the whole group if appropriate.

6. As a part of their English lessons they could be asked to undertake the following tasks

- write down all the words that rhyme
- compose a diary of what has happened in the poem so far, from either the point of view of the owl or the pussycat, or both.

7. As a part of their Art lessons they could draw and paint or colour in the following images

- the owl
- the cat
- the owl strumming his guitar
- the owl and the pussycat sitting in the boat
- the pot of honey.

8. As a part of their History lessons they could study the following

- cats in ancient Egypt
- the owl symbol in ancient Rome.

The Owl and the Pussycat (part 2)

A poem by Edward Lear

> In this activity we continue working on drama ideas for Edward Lear's famous poem and introduce the characters of the pig and the turkey.

Suitable for

KS1, KS2

Cross-curriculum links

Art, English, History

Aims

- To create more character voices.
- To invent frozen tableaux.
- To speak in chorus.

Resources

- Photocopies of the poem

The Owl and the Pussycat (part 2)

They sailed away, for a year and a day,
To the land where the Bong tree grows
And there in a wood a Piggy-wig stood
With a ring at the end of his nose,
    His nose,
    His nose,
With a ring at the end of his nose.

'Dear Pig, are you willing to sell for one shilling
Your ring?' Said the Piggy, 'I will.'
So they took it away, and were married next day

By the Turkey who lives on the hill.
They dined on mince, and slices of quince,
Which they ate with a runcible spoon;
And hand in hand, on the edge of the sand,
They danced by the light of the moon,
The moon,
The moon,
They danced by the light of the moon.

What to do

1. Tell the class that before speaking the second part of this poem they are going to practise the movement of the four animals – the owl, the cat, the pig and the turkey. Key words for each movement could be given as follows

   - (owl) stillness, watchfulness, big eyes, wise
   - (cat) elegance, silence, creeping, calculating
   - (pig) snorting nose, fatness, munching, friendly, stupid
   - (turkey) strutting, long neck, looking from side to side, narrow eyes.

2. Ask the class to get into groups of four. They are now going to practise freezing into the shape of the animal that you call out, so that if you call out 'Owl' all of them have to freeze in the posture of an owl. If you call out 'Pig' they all freeze into the posture of a pig, etc.

   Call out the animals in quick succession, one after the other, and sometimes repeat the same animal quickly.

3. Now ask the groups of four to choose an animal each, and this time when you call out an animal only one person from each group will 'freeze'.

4. Now ask the groups to get into group pictures to denote the following scenes from the poem. Give them thirty seconds to prepare and discuss

   - the owl serenading the cat
   - meeting the pig
   - the pig selling his ring
   - the turkey marrying them
   - them all dancing by the light of the moon.

5. Now practise 'voices' for the various animals. Add the pig and the turkey 'voices' to what you did in the previous activity. Here are some

suggested descriptors, but the children may come up with something better, so let them experiment by themselves to find their 'voices'

- (pig) spluttering, muttering, wobbling voice
- (turkey) precise, boring, fatherly voice.

The turkey will have to invent some dialogue. You could suggest the marriage ceremony lines, 'I now pronounce you man and wife'.

6. Now the children practise reciting the second half of the poem as a group. Once again the whole group will speak in chorus unless the line refers specifically to a character, in which case only that character speaks the line. Let the children work out who speaks which line and then do a 'presentation' to the class with actions and voices.

7. Once the children have got used to the whole story sequence of the poem you could suggest an improvised scenario in which they make up the dialogue themselves using their own words. Although there are, strictly speaking, only four characters in the poem they could be allowed to invent some more characters so that all four of them are involved in every scene. Here is a suggested sequence scenario with extra characters

- (Scene 1) the owl calls on the cat to suggest a picnic. The cat's mother and father are not too happy but eventually allow it.
- (Scene 2) the owl and the pussycat go down to the beach to hire a boat from a boatman and the owl buys a guitar from a salesman in a shop.
- (Scene 3) the owl proposes to the cat and the cat accepts but they realise they have lost their way.
- (Scene 4) eventually they land on the island of the Bong trees and speak to two Bong tree people who direct them to the pig's house.
- (Scene 5) they arrive at the pig's house and buy a wedding ring from the pig; the pig directs them to the turkey/clergyman's house where they will get married.
- (Scene 6) the turkey is not happy about marrying them without their parents' permission but eventually agrees; the pig is best man; they have a party with music afterwards.

Group Sounds (part 1)

In this activity we look at the dramatic effects of making group sounds.

Suitable for

KS1, KS2

Cross·curriculum link

English

Aims

- To listen to each other.
- To watch.
- To be a member of a large team.
- To cooperate.

Resources

- An open space

What to do

1. Ask the class to make the following sounds as a whole group. Tell them that they are to make the 'sound' and try not to use any words at all
   - a whispering sound
   - a shushing sound
   - a hissing sound
   - a mumbling sound
   - a praying sound
   - a muttering sound
   - a grumbling sound.

2. Now the class, still working in chorus, will increase and decrease the volume of the sound. One person can go into the middle of a circle and raise and lower their arms. As they raise their arms the class increase

the volume of the sound and as they lower their arms the class decrease the volume.

3. The class, still standing in a circle, will now act alone in regulating the volume of the sound. Tell them to start the whispering sound very quietly and then everyone will slowly raise their arms. As they raise their arms the volume increases and reaches its loudest when everyone has their arms raised above their heads.

4. If this is successfully accomplished – which requires a lot of concentration – then they can slowly lower their arms and decrease the volume until there is complete silence when their arms are by their sides.

5. Now repeat the whole process incorporating increase and decrease of volume. Try any or all of the above sounds in this way.

6. Place one person in the middle of the circle and tell them that they are having a scary dream. The class starts a sound (say it is the mumbling sound) and as the volume increases the person in the middle acts more and more scared as if these 'sounds' are coming from inside his/her head. Increasing and decreasing the volume will make the person in the middle react. Try different people in the middle of the circle and experiment with different sounds.

7. Split the class up into smaller groups – probably groups of five or six would work best – and give them the following ideas with which to experiment through normal, spoken improvisation. They must however include a central scene that includes a person waking up and hearing 'sounds'

- A person is admitted to hospital and examined by doctors and nurses who say she/he must spend the night in a hospital bed. The patient is awoken at night by strange sounds.
- A group of young people go camping in some woods. At night one of them wakes up in a sleeping bag under a tent and hears strange sounds from the woods outside.
- A person is staying at a remote, creepy hotel in the middle of nowhere. At night she/he is awoken by odd sounds.

Variations

- With item 6 – the scary dream – the class could close in on the 'dreamer' as the volume increases and go out again as the volume decreases.

Group Sounds (part 2)

In this activity we continue experimenting with group sounds in order to make a dramatic impact.

Suitable for

KS1 (optional), KS2

Aims

- To watch carefully.
- To obey a command gesture.
- To work as a chorus.
- To cooperate.

What to do

1. Ask the class to make a group sound to express the following

   - being bored
   - being thrilled
   - being scared
   - laughing at a joke
   - hearing sad news.

2. One of the class goes into the middle of the circle and says the following lines. The group react with the appropriate group 'sound'

   - 'we're all going to visit the museum today!' (class makes bored sound)
   - 'we're all going to Disneyland' (class makes thrilled sound)
   - 'we're going to Dracula's Castle' (class makes scared sound)
   - the person in the middle makes a joke (the class respond by laughing)
   - 'I've failed my exams' (the class makes a sad sound).

3. Here are some further group sounds to make up. Remember that no words must be used, only sounds

- groaning sound as if you are going to be sick
- moaning sound as if you are in pain
- roaring sound as if you are a lion
- cheering sound with clapping
- booing and whistling sound.

4. Place one person in the middle of the circle and decide on a sign or gesture for them to make for the group to start a sound suddenly and end it suddenly. The person in the middle is therefore in control of starting and ending the sound. Decide first of all what sound the group will make and then the group must watch the 'leader' very carefully and wait for the sign to start and finish and then start and finish again. The person in the middle is in control and the group must obey him/her.

5. The whole class must stand in a circle and start a 'humming' sound. They then point with their index finger into the middle of the circle and move in while increasing the volume of the humming. When they are all 'touching fingertips' in the centre of the circle they move back out again while decreasing the volume of the humming. Try this several times until the class are all working and cooperating fully.

6. Ask them to repeat the 'humming' game but this time replace the sound of 'humming' with the sound of 'blowing'.

7. A final very challenging game of group concentration is the 'breathing in and out' game. Make a big circle. The class all 'breathe in' and as they do so they all glide into the centre of the circle and then 'breathe out' as they move backwards to their original positions. Imagine this is like the lungs breathing or a pair of bellows.

8. Ask them to get into groups of five or six and imagine they are some kind of machine breathing in and out. They can make movements as well. Once they have experimented with this idea they will find the whole class exercise much easier.

Variations

- For item 5 you could ask every other person to move into the centre while making the humming sound and then when they move back, the other group move into the centre.
- Another variation for item 5 is to decrease the sound as you move into the centre and increase it as you move outwards.
- In item 8 you could suggest that one of the group is a patient in a hospital and the others are a machine helping him/her to breathe.

Talking in Sounds (part 1)

> In this activity the children will learn to speak using 'sounds' rather than words.

Suitable for

KS2

Cross-curriculum link

English

Aims

- To concentrate and focus attention.
- To experiment with vocal inflections.
- To demonstrate careful listening.

Resources

- An open space

What to do

1. Ask the class to stand in a circle and give them the following 'sounds' to make as a whole group. Ask them to keep repeating the following

   - bla – bla – bla – bla – bla.

2. Ask them now to turn to their neighbours and talk to them using this 'bla – bla' language. They can only say 'bla – bla – bla'.

3. Now tell them to sound surprised using 'bla – bla' language. In the same way, using 'bla – bla' language ask them to sound

   - astonished
   - horrified
   - curious
   - angry
   - friendly.

4. Now they are to work in pairs, so split them all up and ask them to find a space well away from other pairs if possible so that they can concentrate on each other. One of them asks questions in 'bla – bla' language and the other gives answers, also in 'bla – bla' language. The 'questioner' asks the following questions and the other person replies

- ask your partner at what time he/she gets up in the morning on weekdays
- ask your partner at what time he/she gets up at the weekend
- ask your partner when their birthday is
- ask them what they got for their birthday
- ask them who their favourite teacher is
- ask them why
- ask them who their least favourite teacher is
- ask them why
- ask them what their favourite subject is
- ask them what their least favourite subject is
- ask them what they like to eat
- ask them what they don't like to eat.

5. Now that they have got used to talking in 'bla – bla' language arrange for some of the pairs to 'perform' in front of the rest of the class, who have to 'guess' what the questions and replies mean.

6. Another fun exercise to do with this type of work is to ask the 'questioner partner' to speak the questions in English but the answers must always be in 'bla – bla' language. The questioner has to then guess what his/her partner said. Here are some suggested questions to be asked in English

- Where did you go for your holidays this year?
- What do you normally have for breakfast?
- What is your timetable today?
- What programmes do you like watching on TV?
- How many brothers and sisters do you have?
- Describe your mum and dad.

7. Ask them to get into groups of three and devise a 'bla – bla' scene around the following ideas. All of them must speak in 'bla – bla' language

- you arrive home late and your parents tell you off

- you and your friend arrive late for a lesson and the teacher gets cross
- you are all gossiping about a person you hate.

8. Now they can get into larger groups of four or five and attempt the following scenes in 'bla – bla' language

- watching a sporting match on TV with your family and/or friends
- discussing what punishments you were given for not doing homework
- neighbours talking over the garden fence.

Variations

- With item 2 you could also suggest that they speak to people across the other side of the circle and not just to their neighbours.
- While the pairs are talking in 'bla – bla' language you can go round listening to what they are saying and trying to understand the answers.
- In item 4 the pairs can change roles after a set of questions so that it is not always the same person asking the questions.
- In item 4 try to encourage the children to use gesture, movement and facial expression.
- With items 6 and 7 a performance by some of the groups in front of the class would be good fun.

Talking in Sounds (part 2)

> We continue working on more 'sound' language and devise more scenes involving challenging drama games.

Suitable for

KS2

Cross-curriculum link

English

Aims

- To show concentration and focus attention.
- To experiment with vocal inflections.
- To demonstrate careful listening.

Resources

- An open space

What to do

1. After the 'bla – bla' language scenes from the last activity here are some more 'sounds' that can be tried – the children may very well come up with some better ones

    - hoo-ha-hoo-ha
    - bibidi-bibidoo
    - click-clack-click-clack
    - pom-pom-pom-pom-pom.

2. Ask the class to stand in a circle and explain to them that they are going to pass a message round the circle in the language of one of the sounds in item 1. One person starts and then each person passes the same message on to the next person, getting more and more excited. The subject of the messages is as follows

    - (hoo-ha-hoo-ha) I've just seen a ghost in the school library!

- (bibidi-bibidoo) Guess what? There's no school tomorrow because of the bad weather!
- (click-clack-click-clack) I've just heard that Tommy Jones has been sent home for bad behaviour!
- (pom-pom-pom-pom) The school inspectors are coming tomorrow!

3. Once they have got used to 'talking in sounds' ask for some original 'sound' suggestions from the class for passing on a 'big secret' round the circle. Everyone must pass on the message. At the end ask them what the secret was!

4. Ask them to work in pairs or in threes now and work on a sound to advertise a product. Try the following products

- soap
- pens/pencils
- a mobile phone
- an iPod
- a pair of gloves
- chewing gum.

After suitable rehearsal time the teams can perform their adverts in front of the rest of the class.

5. Ask them to sit in a circle and try the following game, which must proceed fairly quickly with no laughing. One person starts with a 'sound' (e.g. hoggy-poggy) and points to someone in the circle who must repeat that sound and then pass on a new one to someone else. If they can't think of a sound they are 'out' and must sit outside the circle. Carry on until there is only one person left, who is obviously the winner.

6. Arrange them into suitable groups to work out the following scenario and act it out using 'sound' language only

A rich, grumpy old man/woman is awoken by a knock at the door. It is two smiling charity workers who are collecting for 'a good cause'.

Grumpy shuts the door and goes back to sleep.

The collectors knock again and insist on some money as they know that grumpy is very rich.

Grumpy threatens to phone the police and the charity collectors finally go away.

Grumpy goes to bed and has a nightmare in which the two charity collectors appear as ghosts saying that he/she will die unless he/she gives some money to charity.

The next day Grumpy goes in search of the charity collectors and gives them all his/her money.

The Daffodils

A poem by William Wordsworth

In this activity we look at a famous poem by Wordsworth and find ways of turning it into drama.

Suitable for

KS1, KS2

Cross-curriculum links

Art, English, History, Geography

Aims

- To learn about punctuation.
- To speak in chorus.
- To stimulate the visual imagination.

Resources

- Photocopies of the poem

The Daffodils

I wandered lonely as a cloud
That floats on high o'er vales and hills,
When all at once I saw a crowd
A host, of golden daffodils;
Beside the lake, beneath the trees,
Fluttering and dancing in the breeze.

Continuous as the stars that shine
And twinkle on the Milky Way,
They stretched in never-ending line
Along the margin of a bay.
Ten thousand saw I at a glance,
Tossing their heads in sprightly dance.

For oft, when on my couch I lie
In vacant or in pensive mood,
They flash upon that inward eye
Which is the bliss of solitude;
And then my heart with pleasure fills,
And dances with the daffodils.

What to do

1. Ask the class to sit in a circle, and give out a photocopy of the poem to each child. Ask them to read round the circle in the following ways

   - one word each
   - one line each
   - between punctuation marks.

2. Split the class into three groups and give each group a verse of the poem. Each group must recite their verse in the following ways

   - as a chorus, all together
   - one line each
   - as a chorus, as fast as possible but keeping together
   - one person recites the verse and the rest of the group speak the last word of each line
   - two people recite the verse and the rest of the group join in on all the rhyming words.

3. Now ask the groups to learn their verse by heart and recite it in any way they like, for example one line each or as a chorus. Have a competition to see which group is the best.

4. Ask the class to find out in which part of England Wordsworth lived.

5. Then they should find a picture of a 'host of daffodils' on the internet and draw or paste it into their exercise book and write out the poem alongside the picture.

6. Get the whole class together and tell them that everyone will be given a role to play in a recitation of the poem. The poem could be recited by one person or by three people – one verse each. The rest of the class will play the following aspects of the poem and will enact through movement and mime what the poem describes. They could either freeze after they've done their part or move continuously

   - the cloud
   - vales
   - a bay
   - heads

- hills
- host of daffodils
- the lake
- the trees
- the breeze
- stars
- the Milky Way
- never-ending line

- dance
- couch
- pensive mood
- inward eye
- bliss of solitude
- heart with pleasure fills
- dancing with the daffodils.

7. Ask the class to look up the dates of William Wordsworth's life and find out something about his history as an English poet.

8. As a part of your Art lessons ask the class to cut out suitable raffia and paper in green and yellow to represent the daffodils and use them in their drama work.

Variations

- There are various visual and aural representations of the poem on YouTube that could be used for research.
- Music would be a helpful accompaniment, especially for item 6. Any of the Chopin nocturnes would be suitable.

Householder

In this activity we play an improvisation game called 'Householder' in which children have to adopt the role of a particular character who calls at a house. The character type is chosen from a card in the character box.

Suitable for

KS2

Cross-curriculum link

English

Aims

- To select a suitable voice to go with a character.
- To sharpen verbal improvisation skills.

Resources

- A character box with cards containing the names of as many types of character as possible
- A door frame with a working door (optional)

What to do

1. In order to get the children into the mood of adopting a multi-role approach to character say that you are going to call out 'character types' from the 'character box' and as soon as you say the word all the children should get into a frozen pose of that character. Try the following characters, but do feel free to add your own

- a gangster
- a soldier
- a doctor
- a plumber
- a hairdresser
- a teacher
- a security guard
- a clown.

2. Now ask the class to get into pairs and this time when you call out the characters they are to 'speak' as the character to each other. In other words there are going to be

- two gangsters talking to each other
- two doctors talking to each other, etc.

3. Now that they have got into the mode of changing characters and accents tell them that they are going to play the game 'Householder'. Set up the door frame (if you have one) and select a child to be 'the householder'. The rest of the class will line up outside the door (which can be mimed) and get ready to knock on the householder's door. Each person is given a card when it is their turn to knock on the door. They must adopt the character of the person on the card and think of a reason why they are knocking on the householder's door. As soon as the householder opens the door the conversation begins. For example

- If the first character, for example, is a 'priest' the conversation can start with 'Hello, I'm your local vicar and I've come to collect some money for the church charity bazaar.'

The conversation between the priest and the householder continues until there is a natural end or if you call out 'cut'. Then a new person goes up and knocks on the door, etc.

4. Another version of 'Householder' could be with 'real-life characters' knocking on the door, either famous TV personalities or sporting personalities or film/pop stars. The children themselves can choose who they want to be when it is their turn.

5. Another version of this type of improvised dialogue could be with fictional characters from books that the children are currently reading, such as Scrooge from *A Christmas Carol* or Fagin from *Oliver Twist*. In this scenario the fictional character can choose who they wish to speak to. For example, Fagin could say, 'I want to speak to Oliver' or Scrooge could say, 'I want to speak to the Ghost of Christmas Past'. The children can use any character from any book they are currently reading and work on an extract from it.

Variations

- Children can be given a character card from the box a few minutes before their turn in order to mentally prepare something.
- As the class get more used to the idea you can give them less and less time to prepare until they get a card just before they knock.
- The householder can be changed after three turns and a new householder chosen.
- Item 5 could be done with pairs of children who are reading the same book rather than the whole class.

Helping Others

In this session we deal with situations that can arise when we are asked to help other people and consider how we should rise to the challenge.

Suitable for

KS2

Cross-curriculum link

English

Aims

- To think quickly.
- To offer suggestions of help.

Resources

- An open space

What to do

1. Give each person in the class a number and make sure that they memorise that number. Ask the class to sit in a big circle. When you call out a number that person has to go into the middle of the circle. Give the person in the middle of the circle a card you have prepared beforehand, which says 'You have forgotten your key and no one is at home'. The person in the middle has to read out what is written on the card. Now call out a number and that person has to go in and help.

   Here are some further suggestions for what could be written on the cards

   - You have sprained your ankle and are in the middle of the countryside while out walking. You have no mobile phone.
   - You are in the middle of nowhere and your car has broken down. You have forgotten your mobile phone.

- The washing machine has just overflowed and no one is at home. The phone is not working.
- You are an elderly person who has dropped all her shopping in the street.

Only one person at a time is allowed to go in to help and you can only help if your number has been called.

2. You can repeat the same situations above but this time up to four people are allowed to go in and help.

3. Put the class into groups of four and give them the following situations, which they must develop as a group. They can choose characters to go with the situation and plan their scenes accordingly. They can use any combination of the following characters to take part in the scene

- mum/dad
- child
- brother/sister
- neighbour
- best friend.

The scene can be based on one of the following situations

- mum has dropped a hot frying pan onto the kitchen floor just after you get back from school
- dad or mum has cut their finger badly while opening a can of beans at lunchtime
- your best friend is going to change schools and you are very sad; you need to talk to someone
- you need help with your homework and ask someone in your family
- the TV has broken and your favourite programme is about to start.

4. In the same groups ask the children to add a second scene to the one they have already created.

5. The groups should then create a scene in which

- you help an elderly person across the road
- you go to the aid of someone who is being bullied
- you help your best friend with their homework
- you help mum or dad to prepare a meal for some visitors
- you offer to clean your classroom at school
- you help put up Christmas decorations at home
- you offer to clean up the house because some of your relatives are coming round for tea.

The Eagle

A poem by Alfred Lord Tennyson

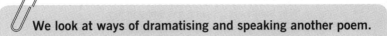

We look at ways of dramatising and speaking another poem.

Suitable for

KS1, KS2

Aims

- To speak clearly as an individual.
- To speak clearly in chorus.
- To use the imagination.
- To demonstrate being still.

Cross-curriculum link

Art

Resources

- Photocopies of the poem

The Eagle

> He clasps the crag with crooked hands;
> Close to the sun in lonely lands
> Ringed with the azure world, he stands.
>
> The wrinkled sea beneath him crawls;
> He watches from his mountain walls,
> And like a thunderbolt he falls.

What to do

1. The class should stand separately and do the following
   - look at their hands
   - imagine their hands are growing old and gnarled
   - imagine claws are growing out of their hands
   - grasp something (not someone!) with their hands and hold on
   - look around
   - imagine their nose is growing like a big beak
   - fix their eyes on something across the room
   - now they are an eagle looking for prey.

2. Go through the above with two or three children only doing the activity and the rest watching. The additional instruction to be given is
   - go for your prey!

3. Ask them to get into pairs. One of them speaks the poem, the other is the eagle.

   The eagle does the movements. Ask them to leave a big dramatic pause after the line:

   > He watches from his mountain walls

   (pause) Then suddenly and dramatically

   > and like a thunderbolt he falls

   The eagle then falls on his prey and gobbles it up!

4. Ask the class to find a picture or an image of an eagle on the internet or do a drawing of one from a book.

5. Get the children into groups of three. Two of them recite the poem in chorus and the third member is the eagle. All have a turn at being the eagle.

6. Have a competition in which the groups have to learn the poem by heart and perform/recite it in front of the whole class.

Shopkeeper

> This is a similar game to 'Householder' in which the children act and speak as characters going into a shop.

Suitable for

KS1, KS2

Cross-curriculum links

English, Mathematics

Aims

- To recognise character from speech patterns.
- To adopt a quick response in improvisation.
- To improve mathematical aptitude.

Resources

- Props such as sweets
- Chocolate
- Toy money or coins

What to do

1. Ask the children to make a list of items they wish to buy from a food shop and to price each item. Add up the total.
2. Ask the class to act going into a shop and buying something. Ask them to work in pairs to begin with. They can choose their own kind of shop. One is the customer, the other is the shopkeeper. They can reverse roles as often as they like. They can work with real props if these are available or just mime.
3. Ask pairs to make a shopping list with a price for each item. The shop is a small general store, not a supermarket. You have to speak

to the shopkeeper, who finds the items for you. Each has a turn as shopkeeper. Add up the total and pay the shopkeeper.

4. Ask them to get into groups of three. One of them is the shopkeeper, two are customers. This is again a small general store where you have to ask the shopkeeper to find the items for you. Both customers have to make up a shopping list with prices and add them up to form a total. These are the characteristics of the customers

   - Customer 1: plain, ordinary, undemanding, slow, agreeable, old
   - Customer 2: snappy, demanding, in a hurry, unpleasant, posh.

5. Ask them now to get into groups of four. One is the shopkeeper. It's a general store, the shopkeeper gets you the items. Each customer makes a shopping list before they go in. These are the characteristics of the customers

   - Customer 1: a gossip, scandalmonger, always moaning about people, especially young people
   - Customer 2: tolerant and mild, puts up with most people, hates arguing
   - Customer 3: a bit snooty, lives in a large house, likes the best of everything and has plenty of money.

Variations

- With item 3 the children can reverse roles as many times as they like.

Spooky Stories

An activity in which we look at unusual stories connected with the supernatural, ghosts and unearthly characters, trying to find the right voice.

Suitable for

KS1 (optional), KS2

Cross-curriculum links

English, History

Aims

- To translate gesture into character.
- To communicate meaning through character.

Resources

- If you have a drama studio with lighting you could try dimming the lights a little
- Plain white masks would be useful if you have them

What to do

1. First of all get the children into a big circle and say that you're going to try out some 'scary' voices. Go round the circle and ask them individually to make the following sounds and then the whole circle repeats the sound
   - an evil laugh
   - a sinister laugh
   - a maniacal laugh
   - a distant laugh
   - a wailing sound
   - a whistling sound
   - a howling sound
   - a breathing sound
   - a growling sound.

2. Now ask them to deliver the following lines in as 'sinister' a voice as they can

- you are my slave, come to me
- beware of the big green dragon
- he eats little boys
- follow, follow, the hollow, the hollow
- creep and sleep, creep and sleep
- abracadabra, abracadabra.

3. Now try the following with the children as a whole class. This can be great fun. Choose one of them to be a magician who will hypnotise the class. 'The magician' can stand on a platform (a chair will do) and move one arm up and down slowly. As they do so, the class will slowly go down on their knees and rise up again. If 'the magician' moves their arm to the left or right, the class sway to the left or right. If 'the magician' beckons the class to come forward, they come forward or back as the magician wills. This can be accompanied by humming sounds from the magician that are echoed by the class.

4. Ask the class to get into groups of five and tell them they are going to work on a scenario called 'The Haunted Hotel'. Here is a list of characters and a plot scenario on which to work. Further details can be added if desired.

The Haunted Hotel (characters)

hotel owner
hotel receptionist
two guests
the 'new' receptionist.

> The guests arrive at the haunted hotel and check in. They are going to stay for only one night. The owner and the receptionist tell them that there is only one room available and it's unfortunately the haunted room. The guests say it does not matter as they do not believe in ghosts.

> They are taken to their room, which has a window at one end and a large wardrobe.

> As soon as they go to sleep they hear a tapping at the window. They wake up but decide it was nothing.

When they go to sleep again they hear a tapping from the wardrobe. They wake up and open the wardrobe but there is nothing there.

They go to sleep again but are awoken by 'sounds' from both the window and the wardrobe. This time they see a ghost at the window and a ghost in the wardrobe.

They rush downstairs but cannot find the owner or the receptionist. A few minutes later the owner and the receptionist appear. They tell their story but the owner and the receptionist tell them not to worry and to go back upstairs again. There are no other rooms available.

The guests go back upstairs and eventually get to sleep. In the morning when they go downstairs they find a new receptionist. The guests ask for the owner and the receptionist they saw last night. The new receptionist tells them that he was on duty last night on his own. They are eventually told that there was an owner who died in a fire two years ago along with a receptionist!

Variations

- As an additional idea you could try reading and working on a lovely comic poem by Charles Causley called 'Colonel Fazackerley'. You can easily find it on the internet and I'm sure the children would love it.
- If the class find item 3 difficult try it in smaller groups to begin with and progress to involving the whole class.

The Land of Counterpane

A poem by Robert Louis Stevenson

> In this poem we recognise what has happened to all of us at one time or another – being ill in bed. What do we do to pass the time?

Suitable for

KS1, KS2

Cross-curriculum link

English

Aims

- To recognise simple everyday events and how to transfer them into drama.
- To create shapes and sounds with the body.
- To use visual imagination.

Resources

- Photocopy of the poem

The Land of Counterpane

When I was sick and lay a-bed,
I had two pillows at my head,
And all my toys beside me lay,
To keep me happy all the day.

And sometimes for an hour or so
I watched my leaden soldiers go,
With different uniforms and drills,
Among the bedclothes, through the hills;

And sometimes sent my ships in fleets
All up and down among the sheets;

Or brought my trees and houses out,
And planted cities all about.

I was the giant great and still
That sits upon the pillow-hill,
And sees before him, dale and plain,
The pleasant land of counterpane.

What to do

1. All sit in a circle and recite the poem, each child reading one line at a time.

2. Go round the circle and ask each child to say the rhyming word in each line.

3. Now go round the circle with each child reading one line again. Start at different places in the circle so that the children will not always have the same line to say.

4. Ask and discuss the meaning of the word 'counterpane'. Ask them what the poem is about.

5. Ask the children to spread out and think of a toy that they could be which might be on the bed. Get into a frozen pose of that toy, then

    - move as the toy
    - stand up as the toy
    - speak as the toy
    - freeze as the toy.
    - fall down as the toy

6. Ask the class to get into the frozen pose of toy soldiers as in verse 2. Repeat the same movements as above.

7. Get them into groups of four or five and ask them to create frozen pictures of a group of toy soldiers. On a drumbeat or a handclap they must come alive and then freeze again on the same signal.

8. Call out and ask the children to get into a frozen pose of the following from verse 3

    - a ship
    - a tree
    - a house.

9. Split the class into three groups. One group represents a ship, another group a tree and another group a house. Ask each group to select various objects, people or things associated with these subjects and then to make up a frozen group picture. After a suitable rehearsal time they must bring the scene to life (with sounds and speech) on a given signal.

10. Now ask them to represent a mixture of objects and people. In groups of five or six, they act out the poem with some of them being objects and some being people

- a narrator who could be the child in bed
- toys
- soldiers
- ships
- trees
- houses.

Eating In and Eating Out

In this session we focus on food and various situations that can arise when we eat at home or eat out at a restaurant.

Suitable for

KS1, KS2

Cross·curriculum link

English

Aims

- To work in a small group.
- To use language clearly.
- To play a role using suitable language.

Resources

- Small tables and chairs

What to do

1. Divide the class into 'adults' and 'children'. The adults have to make sure that the children are using good manners at the table. Pair up the children with an adult and suggest the following situations as the starting point for the parent to give a lesson in good manners

   - how to use a soup spoon
   - how to use a knife and fork
   - how to sit at the table
   - how to speak at the table
   - how to eat a sandwich
   - how to eat breakfast cereal

- how to drink tea
- how to eat cake
- how to drink orange juice.

2. Give the pairs the following situation and ask them to prepare a short dialogue around it.

A very important person is coming round for tea and the adult is giving instructions to the child about how to behave and make an impression. The very important person can be a neighbour who has a bigger house than you.

3. Put the class into groups of three or four and ask them to create a situation in which the very important person comes round for tea. The characters are as follows

- mum
- dad
- child
- rich neighbour.

4. In groups of three or four the children then cast themselves as the following characters in a scene set in a restaurant

- mum
- dad
- child
- snooty waiter/rude waitress.

Try the following scenes using the above characters

- the family go out to a posh restaurant to celebrate the child's birthday; the waiter is very snooty and looks down on them because the family has poor manners
- the family go out to a café for a bite to eat and encounters a very rude waitress who has dreadful manners.

5. In groups of three or four the children cast themselves as the following characters

- mum
- dad
- head waiter
- waiter/waitress.

- In the first scene we see the head waiter giving instructions to his waiter as to how to serve people at table. It is a very posh restaurant.
- In the second scene we see mum and dad entering the restaurant. Mum and dad are celebrating an anniversary. The new waiter is excellent and everything goes well.
- In the next scene, a year later, there is a new waiter who does everything wrong and the evening ends with the waiter getting the sack from the manager.

Waiter, There's a Fly in My Soup!

An activity on improvisations connected with restaurants, cafés and eating!

Suitable for

KS1, KS2

Cross-curriculum link

English

Aims

- To improve timing.
- To learn about comedy effects.

Resources

If possible the following props and furniture would be helpful
- plastic plates, cups and cutlery
- round or square small tables
- tablecloths

What to do

1. Tell the children to get into pairs. They are all going to be waiters/ waitresses and a customer. Call out the following instructions and the children must mime the actions
   - open a door for a customer
   - take them to a table
   - show them a menu

- write down their order
- bring them a drink
- bring them their food
- the customer is not happy
- apologise profusely
- bring them another set of food
- the customer is happy
- they eat their food and drink
- you bring them the bill
- the customer is angry because there is a mistake on the bill
- the customer leaves without paying and you run after them.

2. Ask them now to vocalise the above, both using posh accents. After a suitable rehearsal time each group can show the rest of the class what they have done.

3. The pairs are now both waiters/waitresses, waiting for customers. They are bored and underpaid by their very mean boss. They are speaking about how much they hate their jobs. Suddenly the restaurant is inundated by a crowd of customers and the waiters are plunged into frenetic activity. The two waiters have to serve the customers as fast as they can. They are run off their feet. Finally the customers leave and the two waiters collapse in an exhausted heap.

It is best to do this without other children being customers. The two waiters have to create the impression of a crowd of people.

4. Ask them to get into groups of three and work on the following scenario

Two very lazy waiters/waitresses have joined the staff of a very busy café. The boss comes in and tells them what they are expected to do

- how to greet customers
- how to carry dishes
- how to lay a table
- how to walk properly
- how to be polite to customers when they are being rude.

The boss then insists on being the customer and they must rehearse everything that they have been taught.

5. You can continue to work in the same groups of three or give the children the opportunity to choose another group of three. The following scenario can be worked on

> Two waiters/waitresses are talking about the arrival of a famous film star or pop star who has booked to come to the restaurant. Whatever the waiters say about the film star/pop star is true. For example if the waiters say that the film star has a limp then, when the third person comes in, he or she must limp. Give each group member the opportunity to play the part of the film star.

6. Get the whole class standing in a circle and tell them that they are all restaurant managers. They each have to make a suggestion as to how they would attract customers to their restaurant. For example

- I would have a flashing neon light
- I would have bright orange tablecloths.

If someone cannot think of anything to say they must sit down and are out. The last two people left standing are the best business people.

What Really Annoys Me is ...

In this activity we look at our likes and dislikes and turn them into drama!

Suitable for

KS2

Cross·curriculum link

English

Aims

- To stimulate discussion.
- To learn to express your opinions.

Resources

- An open space
- Pen and paper

What to do

1. Ask the class to sit in a circle. Each person has to say what really annoys them.

2. As a part of English lessons, they write a letter of complaint to the source of their annoyances, whether it be a person or an organisation. Each person can read their letter out loud.

3. Each person has to write down a list of things/people they like and things/people they do not like. They shouldn't speak to anyone about it.

4. Each person reads out what they do *not* like. If there are two or more people who have the same thing written down then they join together as a group. That group then discusses what it is they do not like and must form a decision as to what they are going to do about it.

5. Each person writes a list of things they want and things they don't want. Don't speak to anyone about it.

6. Each person reads out what they do *not* want. If there are two or more people who have (more or less) the same thing written down, join them as a group. Each group should then discuss the matter.

Variations

- With items 3 and 5 you could make up a group of people who agree about what they like and want. They can discuss these in the same way and form a group decision as to what they can do.

Peter and the Wolf

In this activity we look at that wonderful piece of music by Prokofiev called 'Peter and the Wolf' and discover ways of turning the text into drama.

Suitable for

KS1, KS2

Aims

- To adopt frozen poses.
- To speak as a character.
- To move to music.

Cross-curriculum links

English, Music, History

Resources

- Music of Prokofiev's 'Peter and the Wolf'

What to do

1. Tell the children that they are going to learn about an old Russian folk tale called 'Peter and the Wolf'. Before going on to listen to the music and the text ask them to experiment with movements and sounds for the following animals (some of which we have already looked at in Part 1 of the book)

   - bird
   - duck
   - cat
   - wolf.

2. A fun game to get them started would be as follows. The class stand around the edge of the room, facing the walls, with their eyes closed. The teacher goes round the circle and lightly taps every person, saying

'bird', 'duck', 'cat', 'wolf'. Every child will then know what they are. Keeping their eyes closed, the children then have to make the noise of their animal and move towards others who are the same animal as themselves. You could do each animal one at a time or all together. There should eventually be four clusters of each animal. Do the game again, if you like, so that they try a different animal.

3. Ask each animal group to go into a corner of the room. Select someone to be 'Peter', who stands in the centre of the room. Peter calls out any one of the animal groups and they have to go and touch Peter and then go back to their corner, moving as their animal and making the sound of their animal, of course.

4. Now we'll focus on the human characters that appear in the story. Ask the children to get into a 'frozen pose' of

   - a grandfather
   - a hunter
   - Peter.

   Then ask them to 'come alive' and speak by saying something typical of that character. Then go back into a frozen pose, etc.

5. Split the class up into three groups

   - a group of grandfathers
   - a group of hunters
   - a group of Peters.

   Ask each group, one at a time, to move from one side of the room to the other side

   - in slow motion
   - in fast motion
   - in normal motion.

6. Now arrange the class so that they can all see what is happening and have a little competition for the best

   - Peter
   - bird
   - duck
   - cat
   - grandfather
   - wolf
   - hunters.

   You will have to make the decision if it is not obvious who is best.

7. Now tell them that you are going to put on the CD of Prokofiev's 'Peter and the Wolf'. There is music and there is text. Tell the class that they must obey the narrator's instructions as they come up. They can line up according to the order in which they appear. You will already have cast the roles so that when their character comes up they will know who they are and must simply obey the narrator's instructions. The 'actors' must 'move to the music' and imagine what is happening.

8. As a part of their History or Music lessons, ask them to research Prokofiev, the composer, and the story of 'Peter and the Wolf'.

9. As a part of their English lessons, ask them to write a diary account of what happens to Peter on that day.

Variations

- For item 3 you could suggest that the fastest group back to their corner will be the winners.

Television Channels

In this activity children have an opportunity to air their views about their favourite or least favourite TV programmes.

Suitable for

KS1, KS2

Cross·curriculum link

English

Aims

- To stimulate discussion and express points of view.
- To impersonate well-known people.

Resources

- An open space

What to do

1. Ask the children to think of their favourite TV programme, without conferring with each other if possible.
2. Start to ask what their favourite programmes are and sit people together in pairs who have the same opinion.
3. Ask the pairs to discuss the reasons why they have chosen that programme and to prepare a talk based on the following points
   - the content and subject matter
   - the form and structure
   - the actors or presenters.

When the groups are ready they are to present their talks to the rest of the class. At the end of the talk you ask the class for a show of hands as to who has been convinced or not.

4. Ask the class to think of their least favourite TV programme and follow the same procedure as in items 1, 2 and 3.

5. In pairs ask them to choose a TV programme, any programme. One of them is acting on TV and the other is watching. The person watching claps their hands when they want to change channels and the TV person must act out another programme immediately. Keep going until the TV person runs out of ideas!

6. As a part of their English lessons ask them to write a letter of complaint to a TV company about a programme they have watched that they feel is either inappropriate or of a very low standard.

7. In pairs ask them to adopt the roles of

- TV producer
- viewer who complains.

The viewer has been invited to meet the producer of a programme that he or she hates. Ask them to prepare a little scene in which the two meet to discuss the viewer's point of view.

8. In groups of four ask them to choose three television personalities who are interviewed by the fourth person.

Variations

- Item 5 could be played with the whole class watching one person. The teacher changes channels by clapping. Everybody in the class can have a turn at this. The person who manages to act out the most TV programmes convincingly is the winner.
- In item 7 the viewer could meet the producer of a programme they love.

Books

In this activity children enact books and speak in appropriate styles of speech.

Suitable for

KS1, KS2

Cross-curriculum link

English

Aims

- To act as objects.
- To speak in a particular style.

Resources

- An open space
- Different types of book

What to do

1. Ask the children to imagine they are 'books on a shelf'. Ask them to decide how big or small the book is and to all stand in a row on the ground or on a chair.

2. Now ask them to decide what kind of book they are. Give them suggestions such as

   - a dictionary
   - a horror story
   - a romance
   - a glossy art book
   - a reference book

   - a Bible
   - a fantasy
   - a fairy story
   - a poetry book
   - a book of nursery rhymes.

3. Now ask them to think of the very first sentence of the book they represent. When the teacher points to a book 'it' must speak its first sentence.

4. As part of their English lessons they can write the first paragraph of the book they wish to represent or an extract from any book that they like.

5. In the Drama lesson they must read out their extract from their book using an appropriate voice to go with the text.

6. In groups of four ask them to decide on a type of story book – either fantasy, horror, fairy tale, etc. – and to make up one sentence each, continuing the story and then reading it in an appropriate voice for that style of book.

7. In groups of four ask them to imagine that one of them goes into a library and leafs through three books. The three children who are three different types of book must decide on what kind of book they are and speak in an appropriate voice. The person then has to decide which book he or she is going to take out.

Variations

- With item 7 there could be a fifth member of the group who plays a librarian.

Nursery Rhymes

In this activity we look at a popular nursery rhyme and at ways in which we can bring it to life through drama. For more nursery rhymes and historical research into the origins of nursery rhymes you can look at the website www.rhymes.org.uk.

Suitable for

KS1, KS2

Cross-curriculum links

English, History, Art

Aims

- To learn lines by heart.
- To recognise rhymes.
- To plan a scenario in sequence.

Resources

- Website: **www.rhymes.org.uk**
- Copies of specified fairy tales

What to do

1. The following nursery rhyme is completely appropriate for today's children and the issues concerning healthy eating, although the word 'doctor' could be substituted with 'dentist' nowadays.

   An apple a day keeps the doctor away.
   Apple in the morning – doctor's warning.
   Roast apple at night – starves the doctor outright.
   Eat an apple going to bed – knock the doctor on the head.
   Three each day, seven days a week – ruddy apple, ruddy cheeks.

Ask the children to get into pairs and make a list of their five favourite foods and their five least favourite. Each person can read out their list to the rest of the class, who make appropriate sounds of agreement or disagreement in the following ways

- cheer for approval/boo for disagreement
- thumbs up for approval/thumbs down for disagreement
- yum, yum sounds for approval/sick sounds for disagreement.

Ask several of the children to act as survey consultants and make a list of the five favourites and the five least favourites.

2. Give a copy of the nursery rhyme to the class. Ask them to get into pairs and read the rhyme to each other in the following ways

- one line each
- in the voice of an old man or woman
- in the voice of a teacher
- in the voice of a mum or dad
- in the voice of a doctor.

3. In groups of three or four try improvising around the following scenario

A mum or dad reads the nursery rhyme to their two children at bedtime. After the mum and dad leave, the children take out from under their bed one of their favourite – but unhealthiest – foods, and begin to tuck in. They hear the footsteps of mum or dad who are coming back and quickly hide their food. Mum and dad smell something suspicious and when they go out again they wait outside the door, listening. They catch the children red-handed tucking into their favourite food.

They must decide on a healthy food diet for their two children for the foreseeable future and decide to take them to visit the dentist.

4. This scenario could be for groups of three, four or five and could continue from the previous one or be a completely new story

Mum decides it is time for the children to visit the dentist. At the dentist's there is a notice displaying the virtues of eating apples and the dentist is very keen on healthy eating for children. There is also a list of banned foods on the board for example sweets, beefburgers, chips, etc. The children look at the list of banned foods – it contains all their favourites! The dentist looks at their teeth and tells them that their teeth are in an awful state and, unless they change their diet, they will have to have a lot of regular dental treatment. The dentist is a very fierce character and tells off the parents as well as the children. The parents promise to look after their children's diet in a more careful manner in future. The dentist looks at mum's teeth and decides that she will have to have a couple out on the spot as they are so bad. The children rub their hands in glee and secretly eat their favourite food as mum screams with pain!

5. Working in the same way as above, the following nursery rhymes would be suitable for this age group. They all have a historical association that could be studied as a part of their History lessons as well as using them in Drama lessons

- Humpty Dumpty
- Little Miss Muffet
- Pat a cake, Pat a cake
- Pussycat, Pussycat
- This little piggy
- What are little boys made of?

Variations

- In item 4 one of the characters could be a doctor instead of a mum or dad and the children are taken to the doctor for a 'lecture' on healthy eating.
- All the suggested nursery rhymes have the potential to be used as part of Art lessons.

At the Zoo

A poem by William Makepeace Thackeray

In this activity of Part 2 we look at a funny poem by William Makepeace Thackeray, mainly known as a novelist, but who wrote this unusual poem that has so much potential for drama.

Suitable for

KS1, KS2

Cross·curriculum link

Art

Aims

- To mix mime, gesture and voice.
- To practise impersonation.
- To improve memory work.

At the Zoo

First I saw the white bear, then I saw the black;
Then I saw the camel with a hump upon its back;
Then I saw the grey wolf, with mutton in his maw;
Then I saw the wombat waddle in the straw;
Then I saw the elephant a-waving of his trunk;
Then I saw the monkeys – mercy, how unpleasantly they smelt!

What to do

1. As a piece of fun to begin this lesson ask the children to pretend they can suddenly smell something awful in the following ways

   - they enter a room and smell something awful
   - they are sitting down quietly reading and suddenly smell something
   - they are watching television and suddenly smell something awful
   - they are taking a walk in the park and suddenly smell something
   - they are driving a car and suddenly smell something awful
   - they are sunbathing on a beach and suddenly smell something.

   They can do the above one at a time as well as all together. You could have a competition for the best reaction to a bad smell.

2. Now tell them that they will smell something pleasant in the above ways. Again you could have a competition with each child performing one at a time and choose the person who reacted best to the good smell.

3. Divide the class into groups of six. Give them a copy of the poem. They have to read one line each and use their bodies as well as their voices to express the different animals. Ask them to learn their lines by heart and then have a competition for the best group as regards

   - knowing it by heart
   - best mime
   - best vocal interpretation.

4. Ask the groups to recite the poem as a chorus. They must learn the whole poem by heart and use mime, gesture and vocal variation to express the meaning of the poem. Each group performs in front of the whole class after suitable rehearsal time.

5. Now tell the groups that they must choose one person to be narrator and read the poem out loud. The other people in the group will be cast as the various animals

   - white bear
   - wolf
   - black bear
   - wombat
   - camel
   - elephant

   Everyone can join in and be monkeys!

6. Get the class to look up images of all the animals mentioned in the poem and draw and colour in each one.

7. Go round the class and name each person as a different animal from the poem.

As the teacher calls out the name of an animal the group of children have to come together as a herd and make the appropriate movement and sound of the animal. Call out the animal names quite quickly. When it is not their turn they must freeze.

Victorian Children up Chimneys

In this activity we learn a little about how poor Victorian children were used as cheap labour and how drama can be used to examine historical issues.

Suitable for

KS1, KS2

Cross-curriculum links

English, History

Aims

- To develop a sense of history by looking at photographs of Victorian children in the workplace.

Resources

- Use of computer facilities

What to do

1. Organise children into groups of four to discuss the following statement

   Children were often forced to work almost as soon as they could walk. This was not something new to the Victorian period as children had always been expected to work for hundreds of years. Many were used as cheap labour.

   Consider the following questions

   - In what ways were children expected to work?
   - From what age?
   - What kind of work were children expected to do?
   - What kind of hours did they work?

- Why were children exploited in this way?
- What kind of protection did they have in law?
- How could children escape from this kind of work?
- What was the reason they could be exploited in this way?
- How could their parents protect them?
- Describe in your own words how you would feel about being sent up a chimney.

2. Chimney sweeping was a job children could do better than adults. Small boys (starting at the age of five or six) would be sent scrambling up inside the chimney to scrape and brush soot away. They came down covered in soot, and with bleeding elbows and knees.

> *I have two boys working for me. After work their arms and legs are bleeding so I rub them with salt-water before sending them up another chimney.* Sweep

Ask the children to get into groups of three. They should attempt to devise a scene in which the master sweep tells them what is expected of them. Here are some questions and statements the master could put to the two children

- How old are you lads?
- Where have you worked before?
- What work do your parents do?
- Where do you live?
- I'll be relying on you to do a good job and no complaints!
- If you get stuck up that chimney don't expect me to come up and get you down.
- If you want to be paid you'll have to do a good job.
- We've got three chimneys to sweep today so look sharpish!
- If you do a good job I'll give you a bit of bread and dripping.
- If you 'urt yourselves I'll rub salt into your wounds, which will sting something 'orrible so don't get 'urt.
- If you please me today I may employ you again tomorrow!
- If you get stuck up the chimney I'll have to light a fire, so that should get you down!

3. In groups of three or four ask the children to devise a scene between children and their parents at home after a day's work. Here are some pointers to what the parents might say

- What happened to you today?
- What was the master sweep like?
- Did he pay you and how much?
- How many chimneys did you clean today?
- What were the houses like that you worked in?
- Did he give you anything to eat?
- I suppose you'll want a bath, well that costs money so you'll have to give me all your wages.

Variations

- The children could carry out further research on the subject by consulting the following resources
  - www.chiddingstone.kent.sch.uk/homework/victorians/children/working.htm
  - *Pit Boy* by Gordon Ottewell (Green Branch Press, 2012).

Victorian Children in Factories

We continue in this activity to look at the employment of children in Victorian times and find ways of using drama to express some historical themes.

Suitable for

KS1, KS2

Cross-curriculum links

History, English

Aims

- To develop a sense of history by looking at photographs of Victorian children in the workplace.

Resources

- Use of computer facilities

What to do

1. I start work promptly at five in the morning and work all day till nine at night. That's 16 hours! We are not allowed to talk, sit or look out of the window whilst we work. The only day off from work I get is on Sundays, when we have to go to church. (Girl, aged nine)

    In pairs ask the children to create a conversation between two children who work in a factory, using the above statement as a starting point.

    Bring the following points of interest into the conversation

    - you work in a textile mill where some jobs are very dangerous
    - you have to clean the machines while they're still running
    - you crushed your hand in the machinery recently

- one of your friends was killed
- another friend of yours lost their fingers
- children are much cheaper than adults
- children can be replaced from orphanages
- children are small enough to crawl under machinery to tie loose threads
- from 1833 it became illegal to employ children under nine in textile factories.

2. In match factories children were employed to dip matches into a dangerous chemical called phosphorous. The phosphorous could cause their teeth to rot and some died from the effect of breathing it into their lungs.

In groups of four ask the children to create a scene in which four children are discussing the dangers of working in a 'match factory'. Mention all the following points in the conversation

- the long hours
- it's cheaper to employ children rather than adults
- dipping matches into a dangerous chemical called phosphorous
- this can cause teeth to rot
- breathing it into your lungs can cause death
- your living conditions at home
- your parents working long hours
- how you long for some decent food
- factory owners put profit before safety
- how you envy the children of rich parents who can afford nice clothes.

3. In early Victorian England, most children never went to school at all and grew up unable to read or write. Instead they were sent out to work to earn money for their families. Only the upper- and middle-class children went to school.

Now the children can create a conversation with a partner in which one of them is poor and the other rich. If you were poor in early Victorian England you had to work in a factory and earn a living while a rich person had a governess who taught them at home up to the age of ten.

In this conversation one partner is a chimney boy who is having a short break and the other is the son of the owner, who comes in to get a book from the room. Bring the following points into your conversations

- the rich boy asks what you are doing here
- you explain who you are
- the rich boy asks what you are eating
- you show him your bread and dripping
- the rich boy says you smell and you are dirty
- you explain that you have to go up the chimney to clean it
- the rich boy asks if you go to school
- you say you cannot read
- the rich boy shows you a book
- you say you cannot understand it
- the rich boy asks where you live
- you tell him you live in a slum, not a grand house like this
- the rich boy asks how many rooms there are in your house
- you say only one
- you ask to get back up the chimney or else your master will beat you
- the rich boy wants to go up the chimney too
- you try to stop him
- you have a fight
- the master chimney sweep come in!

Variations

- The children could carry out further research on the subject by consulting the following resources
  - www.chiddingstone.kent.sch.uk/homework/victorians/children/working. htm
  - *Pit Boy* by Gordon Ottewell (Green Branch Press, 2012).

Part 3
Character

Character

The third part of the book puts movement and speech together to create character. This means that children are given the opportunity to work on developing what they have learnt in Parts 1 and 2 by extending their performance skills and learning to work as performers communicating meaning through characterisation. There are scripts available online that refer to certain activities in this part and though it is not essential to use them it would be useful to access them and decide if they might be appropriate for your pupils.

It would be a way of introducing the children to quality literature – including Dickens and Shakespeare – where they can gain additional insight into the communicative power of drama.

Oliver Twist (The Board)

This activity refers to the dramatised extract from Oliver Twist called 'The Board' in which young Oliver is taken by Mr Bumble to be presented to a group of rather unpleasant characters who form a board of directors who will decide Oliver's future. There are many opportunities here for creating character types through movement and vocal work.

Suitable for

KS2

Cross-curriculum links

English, History, Art

Aims

- To develop character types through movement.
- To focus on the use of gesture.
- To learn key words in describing character.
- To research some ninteenth-century costumes.
- To understand how props can be an aid to character.

Resources

- Three desks and three chairs
- Some simple props such as gloves, scarves, trays, hats, briefcases
- Some books on Victorian costume
- Notebooks for research notes
- Script of *Oliver Twist* ('The Board') available online (optional)
- DVD of *Oliver Twist* directed by David Lean (optional)

What to do

1. Start by asking the children to move and walk as the following types of character
   - a rich person
   - a poor person
   - a beggar
   - a pickpocket
   - a well-fed person
   - a hungry person
   - a bully
   - a victim.

2. Ask them to add a voice to their character movement and make up a typical sentence that the character might say.

3. Ask them to add a gesture to their character that will typify the essence of the character, for example folded arms, pointing with index finger, showing palms of hands, etc.

4. Place them in groups of two and ask them to improvise a scene between
   - a rich person and a beggar
   - a well-fed person and a hungry one
   - a bully and a victim
   - a master and a servant.

   Suggest that they think about the place in which the scene is set before they start to rehearse.

   Ask them to perform their scenes in front of the rest of the class if they wish.

5. Ask the class to write down in their notebooks the key words, phrases and sentences that best represent the different types of characters they have created.

6. Ask them to describe what their character might be wearing and what they might be carrying. Try to use some simple props and accessories, such as hats, briefcases, scarves, gloves, etc.

7. If you have chosen to use the online script of *Oliver Twist* ask the class to do some research into Victorian costume and perhaps download an image of Mr Bumble, young Oliver and a wealthy Victorian person.

Variations

- Some mime work may be helpful as an additional stimulus to characterisation. For example they could try the following mimes as a poor servant
  - polishing a wooden floor
  - sweeping the cellars
  - scrubbing stone steps
  - mopping a kitchen floor
  - vacuuming a carpet
  - dusting an expensive vase
  - gathering leaves into bags
  - stirring soup.
- You could then ask them to mime the following as a rich person
  - drinking a cup of tea
  - walking through their garden
  - looking at their house
  - standing in front of the fireplace
  - patting their dogs
  - giving an order to a servant
  - sitting comfortably
  - giving a donation to charity.

Oliver Twist (Picking Straws)

This activity refers to the scene from *Oliver Twist* in which the children in the workhouse are deciding who should ask for more food. The scene can be accessed on the website.

Suitable for

KS1 (optional), KS2

Cross-curriculum links

English, History

Aims

- To portray character through movement and voice.
- To work with accents.
- To group mime.

Resources

- Access the script of *Oliver Twist* – ('Picking Straws')
- Internet research on nineteenth-century workhouses
- White card to act as straws

What to do

1. Ask the class to walk around the room in the following ways

   - as if they were cold
   - as if they were very cold
   - as if they were freezing
   - as if they were hot
   - as if they were very hot
   - as if they were boiling
   - as if they were tired

- as if they were very tired
- as if they were totally exhausted
- as if they were poor
- as if they were very poor
- as if they were a beggar.

2. Get them into pairs. They are going to make up an improvised scenario with their partner in which they are two poor beggars on the streets. A third person can join them to play the small part of the rich person

- they are both cold and miserable
- they look through a window and see a family tucking into a hot meal by a roaring log fire
- they fall asleep and imagine they are in the room
- they wake up and find themselves on the street again
- they decide to knock on the door and ask for some food
- a rich person opens the door
- what happens next?

3. Get the class into groups of four/five. They are poor orphans in a workhouse in nineteenth-century London. They are cold, tired, dirty and hungry. They have had a meal but it's not enough. They have to choose someone to be a spokesperson and ask for more food. What method do they use to choose the spokesperson?

4. **a.** In their groups they read the scene from *Oliver Twist* and decide who is going to play the various parts. You could suggest the following casting rules

- Oliver should be the smallest
- pauper 1 should be the tallest
- pauper 2 should be the youngest
- pauper 3 should be the oldest
- pauper 4 should be the biggest.

b. Try the following suggestions for communicating the idea of hunger

- all repeat the word 'beef'
- all repeat the word 'sprouts'
- all repeat the word 'potatoes'
- all repeat the word 'carrots'
- all repeat the words 'lovely juicy gravy'.

c. In order for the children to understand the tension of 'picking the straws' you should provide some thin card and cut them mainly equal with a few short ones. Each member of the group of five has a go at holding the 'straws' and everyone picks one. The one with the shortest 'straw' has to perform a silly-looking task, for example

- stand on one leg with finger in ear for thirty seconds
- hands on head sitting on the floor for thirty seconds
- lying on your back with hands in the air for thirty seconds
- any other silly things that the group or you decide.

d. Now they practise the following scenarios in their groups and cast the parts as they wish. You can arbitrate if there is a dispute about allotting roles

- a strict mum and dad with three children who have to decide who is going to ask for more pocket money
- a strict mum and dad with three children who have to decide who is going to confess to having broken a window
- a strict mum, dad and gran with two children who have to decide who is going to have the courage to tell the grown-ups that they have failed their exams at school
- a very strict mum whose four children have to confess that one of them has broken a priceless vase.

5. Now they should be in a position to act out the scene from 'Oliver' in their groups and perform it for the rest of the class, with costumes and props if these are available.

Variations

- It might be helpful for everyone to experiment with the following mime ideas at some point in the 'Oliver' session
  - eating a delicious bowl of soup and being satisfied at the end
  - eating a small bowl of nice soup but still being hungry at the end
  - eating a disgusting bowl of soup but finishing it because you are so hungry.
- You could also experiment with the following vocal work for this session. The following are spoken by one person in a whining voice and then the rest of the group repeats

- I'm so hungry!
- I'm so unhappy!
- I'm so cold!
- I'm so poor!
- Where's my mummy?
- I'm so thirsty!
- I'm so scared!
- I'm going to be killed!
- I'm going to be murdered!
- I'm going to be flayed alive!
- Where's mummy?

Oliver Twist (Meeting his New Employer)

> In this activity we work on the scene in which Oliver is brought by Mr Bumble to work for Mr Sowerberry, the undertaker.

Suitable for

KS1 (optional), KS2

Cross-curriculum link

English

Aims

- To show physical representation of character.

What to do

1. Read the scene with the class.

2. Ask the children to walk in the following ways
   - as a fat person
   - as a very fat person
   - as an enormously fat person
   - as a thin person
   - as a very thin person
   - as a skeleton.

3. In this scene from *Oliver Twist* the children try to think of the characters as being either fat or thin. Write down what you think
   - Mr Bumble is
   - Mr Sowerberry is
   - Mrs Sowerberry is
   - Charlotte is
   - Noah Claypole is
   - Oliver is.

4. Call out each of the above names and ask the class to walk as that character.

5. Give out a card to each person in the class. On each card is written one name
   - Bumble
   - Charlotte

- Sowerberry
- Mrs Sowerberry
- Noah Claypole
- Oliver.

Call out the name of one of the characters and each person who has that card has to walk as that character. For example if you call out 'Bumble' each person who has a 'Bumble' card has to stand and walk as Mr Bumble.

6. Do the same but this time they must talk as the character. You give them a sentence for each character as follows

- Bumble – 'The boy's a fool'
- Mr Sowerberry – 'A most decent day's business'
- Mrs Sowerberry – 'He's a bit small'
- Charlotte – 'Who shall I say is calling, sir?'
- Noah – 'Just you remember your respect for me, you brat.'
- Oliver – 'Don't you dare talk about my mother.'

7. You can make up fun games using these character cards

- all Bumbles sit
- Charlottes bow
- Mrs Sowerberrys shake hands with each other
- Olivers 'ask for more'
- Noah Claypoles raise their fists
- Mr Sowerberrys lie as if in a coffin.

8. Further variations could be

- Bumbles shake hands with Sowerberrys
- Charlottes bow to all Mrs Sowerberrys
- Noah Claypoles push Olivers.

Oliver Twist (Meeting Fagin)

In this activity Oliver meets Fagin and learns how to become a pickpocket. The drama lesson focuses on the idea of the world of adults and the world of children.

Suitable for

KS1 (optional), KS2

Cross-curriculum link

English

Aims

- To show character interpretation.
- To take characters and situations from the past and update them.

Resources

- Pencil and paper

What to do

1. The scripted extract has four characters. There are three children (Oliver, Dodger, Charlie Bates) and an adult (Fagin). Ask the class to get into groups of four. Ask each group to write down what they think are the differences between the adult world and the child's world.

2. After a suitable discussion ask them to write down what the differences would be in acting out adult characters and children in terms of voice, movement and character.

3. One of the group must volunteer to be an adult. Now give them the following ideas with which to experiment in improvisation

   - three naughty children and a harassed mum in a supermarket
   - three naughty children and a strict mum at the dinner table

- three naughty children and a harassed teacher in the playground
- three naughty children and a strict teacher in a Maths class.

4. If suitable the above could be performed in front of others before moving on to the next set of adults and children

- three well-behaved children with mum at the cinema
- three well-behaved children with mum in the library
- two naughty children and one well-behaved child with mum in the cinema
- two naughty children and one well-behaved child with mum in the library.

5. Now the children and the adult will not be members of the same family. Work on the following ideas

- three naughty children at a fairground and a fairground attendant
- three naughty children in a museum and a museum attendant
- three naughty children in a shopping centre and a policeman
- three naughty children in a cinema and the cinema manager.

6. Now get them to read the extract from *Oliver Twist* in their groups. Ask them to sort out who will play Fagin by each having a turn at reading the part. When the groups have decided on who will play the parts ask them to concentrate on the following

- Fagin is looking at his jewels
- the boys appear outside the door
- the knock at the door
- Fagin is startled
- Fagin hides his jewels.

The dialogue starts.

7. Work on the following scenario as a mime improvisation

- a rich gentleman is standing in a bookshop, reading a book
- two little thieves appear
- they see his wallet sticking out of his back pocket
- they approach the gentleman
- one of them gently takes the wallet and passes it to the other
- the rich gentleman feels for his wallet and discovers it has gone
- he looks round and grabs an innocent boy standing next to him
- the real thieves run off.

8. In their groups they now practise stealing the following items from someone. Try to use the real thing if you can

- a £5 note
- a watch
- a mobile phone
- an iPod
- a handbag
- an apple
- someone's packed lunch.

9. In groups of three they mime the scene in which the boys steal Oliver's handkerchiefs, but in slow motion.

The Secret Garden (Mary Lennox in India)

In this activity we look at the first part of the dramatisation of *The Secret Garden*, which is available to view and copy on the website. Many of the activities, however, can be done without reference to the script.

Suitable for

KS2

Cross-curriculum link

English

Aims

- To marry mime and narration.
- To represent character in a physical way.

Resources

- CD of Indian flute music

What to do

1. Narration is an important part of drama and is used by dramatists and film makers all the time. Here are some examples of how narration can work in a simple story. Get the class into pairs. One is narrator and the other provides the action. The narrator speaks the following and the 'actor' acts out the 'action' with body and voice as necessary

  - Billy Piper got up every morning and threw open the curtains. He then went into the bathroom and looked at himself in the mirror. He touched the scar on his forehead where he had had a fight the previous day and said to himself that he would never get into a fight with a bigger person ever again.

- Jenna was looking at her toys one by one. She picked up the rag doll and put it down again. She picked up her favourite teddy bear and held it closely. She looked at it affectionately. She then heard the familiar voices of her parents rowing and thought to herself, 'I'm not going to take any notice.'

2. Ask the pairs to write a piece of narration about a slice of action from a sporting event. When they have finished they can act it out in the same way as above.

3. In the same way they read and act out the narration from *The Secret Garden* with one of them as narrator and the other as Mary.

4. The whole class can sit in a circle and read the narration from *The Secret Garden* in the following ways

   - each person reads one sentence
   - each person reads up to the next punctuation mark
   - each person reads a section that contains one verb only.

5. As a bad-tempered little girl Mary Lennox was not very popular. Let them try the following actions as a bad-tempered person

   - walk in a bad temper
   - sit in a bad temper
   - open a door in a bad temper
   - stamp in a bad temper
   - shout in a bad temper.

6. Get them into pairs. One is a bad-tempered person and the other is an adult with authority so that the bad-tempered person cannot have his/ her way. The bad-tempered person can only fume and sulk. Now they try the following scenario improvisations

   - a strict teacher tells off a bad-tempered person for bullying other pupils
   - a strict parent tells off a bad-tempered son/daughter for bullying a younger brother or sister.

7. Everybody has now to concentrate on the military soldiers in the extract and try to read their lines with the appropriate posture and voice. They should try the following actions first of all

   - walking as if wearing a tight uniform
   - marching in a tight uniform

- standing upright to attention and saluting
- marching upright looking to the left
- marching upright looking to the right
- marching, stopping, taking out their sword.

Both soldiers are officers so they will be very well-spoken, with 'educated' voices. The class try saying the following lines as if to a parade of a hundred soldiers

- By the left, quick march!
- Halt!
- Stand to attention!
- Stop talking in the ranks!
- You're a disgrace, the lot of you!

8. Now we are going to concentrate on the little boy, Basil, who is only seven years old, and his conversation with Mary. The children should find a partner who is either taller or shorter than them and try the following exercises before reading the whole dialogue

Basil: You smell!
Mary: So do you!

Basil: You're a girl!
Mary: So are you!

Basil: You know nothing!
Mary: Nor do you!

Basil: You're mad!
Mary: So are you!

Basil: I can't stand you!
Mary: I can't stand *you*!

Basil: You're a bean pole!
Mary: You're a shrimp!

Basil: Get lost!
Mary: Get lost yourself!

Now they read the dialogue between Mary and Basil in the script.

9. In groups of four or five they try to learn the chant 'Mistress Mary, quite contrary' by heart and then choose one of the group and taunt them with it in the following ways

- starting softly and getting louder
- walking slowly towards Mary
- surrounding Mary
- with Mary sitting on the floor.

10. In pairs look at the dialogue between Mr and Mrs Crawford. There is no need to read it as written for this exercise. Try reading one sentence each in the following ways

- in hushed whispers
- loudly at dinner
- to your hairdresser
- to a priest.

11. Now that they are familiar with the extract, try casting it and reading the whole extract in preparation for a performance. The narrator's lines should be shared amongst a number of people so that everyone in the class will have a part to play.

12. Rehearsals could be conducted in groups as follows

- the narrators
- officers and Mrs Lennox
- Mr and Mrs Crawford
- Mary and Basil.

Variations

- If there is an odd person left over for item 3 there can be two narrators who read alternate lines.
- With item 9 you could get the whole class to taunt Mary with the chant of 'Mistress Mary'.
- A CD of Indian flute music would help with the atmosphere of this scene.

The Secret Garden (Mary Lennox in England)

In this activity we continue exploring character with another episode of *The Secret Garden*. Mary arrives in England to be taken by train to Yorkshire. She is accompanied by Mrs Medlock, the housekeeper from Misselthwaite Manor.

Suitable for

KS2

Cross-curriculum link

English

Aims

- To represent character in physical terms.
- To use props and accessories to best effect.

Resources

- A bonnet (or several bonnets) for Mrs Medlock
- A coloured ribbon for Mary's hair
- Sound effects of a steam train

What to do

1. Mary does not want to be seen with Mrs Medlock because she considers her to be a servant and therefore inferior. As a child of ten, Mary must come across to the audience as a very proud, arrogant and thoroughly dislikeable little girl. She is not a sympathetic character at all at this early stage, therefore the acting challenge is to find ways of communicating this to an audience.

Ask the children to find a space where they are in isolation. Look at other people in the class

- with hatred
- as if they are inferior
- frown at them
- ignore them
- look away again
- turn your back on them
- as if they are scum.

2. Now we continue with ways of communicating an unsympathetic, fiercely superior character. All the children walk round the classroom in the following ways

- ignoring everyone else
- going in the opposite direction as soon as you come across anyone
- when you come across anyone, look them up and down and then walk on
- say 'good morning' to people as you pass by them but do not stop.

3. Divide the class into two. Half the class play the role of Mary and the other half are Mrs Medlock. They all walk around and when 'the Marys' come across a 'Mrs Medlock' they say the following to her and walk on

- Where is my luggage?
- Fetch my luggage at once!
- Don't dawdle!
- I don't want to be seen with you!

4. Ask the children to find a partner. One of them is master and the other is a servant. Masters give the servants orders about the following

- what you would like for lunch
- how to clean your room
- what you would like to wear today
- arrangements for travel.

5. Now ask all the 'Mrs Medlocks' to pair up and all 'the Marys' to pair up. Each pair should attempt to improvise a conversation in which they talk about their mistress or their servant. Ask if any pair would like to perform their conversation in front of the class after suitable rehearsal time. The subject of their conversations can follow the pattern of item 4.

6. Ask them to get into groups of three. One is narrator, the other is Mary and the last one is Mrs Medlock. The narrator reads the narration passages in the extract and Mary and Mrs Medlock have to act out what is spoken by the narrator.

7. Ask them to get into suitable pairs to read the dialogue between Mrs Medlock and Mary in the train.

8. As a part of their English lessons ask them to make two lists. One list must contain all the words and phrases that refer to Mrs Medlock and the other list all the words and phrases that refer to Mary. For example under 'Mary' you could start with 'she's a plain little piece of goods'. This gives you a clue as regards acting the character. They could work with the same partner as they had in item 7.

9. If you have a sound effects CD of a steam train ask the children to speak their lines as follows

- loudly enough to be heard above the noise
- moving with the motion of the train.

Variations

- In item 3 it would be a good idea to find a way of identifying the 'Mrs Medlocks' by giving the children a prop such as a bag or a satchel or some other means of identification. If possible bonnets would be most suitable.

The Secret Garden (Arrival at Misselthwaite Manor)

In this activity we focus on the extract in which Mary Lennox arrives at Misselthwaite Manor in Yorkshire and we do some Geography.

Suitable for

KS2

Cross-curriculum links

Geography, English

Aims

- To improve knowledge of geography of the British Isles.
- To represent character through simple props.

Resources

- Maps of the British Isles
- Sound effects of wind
- Sound of carriage and horses
- Station master's hat if possible

What to do

1. Give each person in the class a map of the British Isles in which all the counties are clearly indicated. Ask them to find Yorkshire and to trace the journey of Mary and Mrs Medlock from London to the Yorkshire Moors. Get them to draw a map of the journey, colouring in the beginning and end of the journey.

2. Give them the following tasks, which can be tackled in pairs if so desired

   - trace possible routes, by rail and road, to Yorkshire from where they live

- find out how far it is, in miles and kilometres, to Yorkshire from London
- how far is it from where you live?
- in which part of Yorkshire are the moors?
- calculate how long it takes to get from London to Yorkshire now
- calculate how long it took Mary and Mrs Medlock.

3. Ask them to find images of the Yorkshire Moors to understand why Mary thinks it is like 'the sea'.

4. A game of 'Go There' can be great fun and give the children a sense of the geography of the British Isles

   - draw on the floor of the drama room or indicate with chairs the following areas in the UK – Scotland, Wales, Yorkshire, London, the Midlands, the South West
   - split the class up into six groups and place each group in one of the areas
   - call out – for example – 'Scotland to Wales!' This means that the Scotland group must all move to the Wales area. Then you could call out – for example – 'Wales to London'. Continue calling until they have a good sense of where to go. They could all end up in Yorkshire!

5. A big map on a wall on which counties are clearly marked could also serve as a good game to teach Geography. An outline of the British Isles should also be drawn or marked on the drama room floor. Again place groups (or individuals) in different counties and then call out – for example – 'Devon to Lancashire' and point with a big pointer at the map on the wall. The person (or group) who is in Devon must then move to Lancashire. Continue calling until everyone has moved and go as fast as you can to keep everyone on the move. All could end up in Yorkshire again!

6. Put on a CD of the sound of the wind blowing and ask the children to gather in the centre of the room and mime as follows

   - they are all in the middle of the Yorkshire Moors
   - everyone is waiting for a bus
   - everyone is cold
   - everyone is frightened
   - everyone is hungry
   - everyone is miserable

- everyone is looking for the bus
- everyone is getting impatient
- they see something in the distance
- it is *not* the bus
- they start to argue about the queue
- someone sees the bus
- they all cheer.

7. Get them into groups of three. One of them is Mary, another is Mrs Medlock and the third is the station master. Read the script together. The station master has a strong accent. It can be a Yorkshire or any other accent – as long as it is not standard English it can be any accent or dialect from any part of the British Isles. The station master is

- old
- grumpy
- bad-tempered.

They should learn the lines by heart and do the scene as a performance.

8. In the same groups of three they read the scene where they arrive at Misselthwaite Manor and are greeted by Pitcher, the manservant. Again the manservant should have an accent. The manservant could be

- very old
- very grumpy
- very bad-tempered.

Again they should learn the lines by heart and do the scene as a performance.

9. In groups of three ask them to look at the scene in which Mary mimes walking through Misselthwaite to get to her room. This scene is to indicate how vast the house is – a hundred rooms! One of the group is the narrator. Mrs Medlock and Mary walk down corridors and up staircases together, as described by the narrator, until they get to Mary's room. Mrs Medlock says her line and that is the end of the scene. The narrator can add some more directions, as follows

- walked along a large landing
- went up a big staircase
- turned left into a vast hallway
- went through a narrow corridor

- opened a heavy door
- walked through a room that curved to the right.

10. Ask the children to write an extract from Mary's diary in which she describes her thoughts about the following aspects of her journey from London

- the train station in London
- the train carriage
- Mrs Medlock
- the weather
- the Yorkshire Moors
- arrival at Thwaite Station
- the station master
- the carriage drive to the Manor
- Pitcher
- walking to her room.

Variations

- If item 6 is not practical for the whole class then you could do it in smaller groups, but ensure that the groups have their own clearly delineated area.
- With item 5 you could make it more complicated by telling them to go via a certain area – for example – 'From Cornwall to Yorkshire, via London'.

The Secret Garden (At Misselthwaite Manor)

In this activity Mary meets Martha, the housemaid, and learns that life in England is going to be very different from life in India.

Suitable for

KS2

Cross-curriculum link

English

Aims

• To focus on facial expression.

Resources

• Props – a large old-fashioned key

What to do

1. Ask the class to get into pairs and read through the passage 'At Misselthwaite Manor'. Remind them that Martha, the housemaid, is not much older than Mary so it is like two children talking except that Martha is much more mature. Make two lists

   • all the things that Mary finds strange and difficult to get used to
   • the advice that Martha gives her.

2. Still in their pairs, both write up a diary of what each thinks of the other. You can call it 'Mary's Diary' and 'Martha's Diary'.

3. Give the class the following set of comprehension questions, which can be done either orally or as a set of written answers

   • What is the first thing that Mary sees when she wakes up?

- Why does Martha love the moor?
- Whose servant is Martha?
- Why does Mary expect to be dressed?
- What is an 'ayah'?
- Why does Mary get so angry when Martha thought her 'a native'?
- What do we learn about Martha's family?
- What does Martha say Mary will have to get used to?
- What is 'the secret garden'?

4. Ask the children to spread out and lie down on the floor. Just as Mary wakes up in a strange new room tell the class that they are going to wake up and react to the following stimuli

- wake up and see familiar surroundings
- look at your familiar clock
- look at your familiar pictures/posters on the wall
- go and pull your familiar curtains
- look at you familiar view.

Now they wake up and see unfamiliar surroundings and objects

- look at an unfamiliar clock
- look at unfamiliar pictures on the walls
- go to unfamiliar curtains and pull them
- you see an unfamiliar view.

5. They get back into pairs again and read the opening to Episode 4 of *The Secret Garden*. One of them reads the narrator's part and the other is Mary. Mary 'acts out' whatever the narrator says. Ask them to swap roles so that they both have a go at being Mary.

6. Martha says that Mr Craven locked up the garden and buried the key. Using a real key the class can play 'Find the Key'. One person is chosen to go outside the room and the class hide a key somewhere. The person comes in and tries to find the key. The class can make the following sound effects – becoming louder or quieter – to give a clue as to whether the person is getting closer or further away from the key

- a humming sound that gets louder as the person gets closer to the key
- a clapping sound that gets louder as the person gets closer to the key
- a chanting of 'Mistress Mary, quite contrary, how does your garden grow?' from Episode 1.

A Midsummer Night's Dream (Supernatural Characters)

In this activity we look at how to play 'other-worldly' characters and take a few examples from Shakespeare's play. It would be best if the children were shown one of the film versions on DVD.

Suitable for

KS1, KS2

Cross-curriculum link

English

Aims

- To act in a larger than life manner.
- To speak clearly.
- To project character through movement.

Resources

- A CD of Wagner's 'Die Walküre'
- A CD of thunder and lightning sound effects
- A DVD of *A Midsummer Night's Dream*
- A CD of *Lord of the Rings*

What to do

1. Oberon and Titania are the King and Queen of the Fairy Kingdom. They are supernatural characters who cannot be played like ordinary mortals, therefore we have to look at ways of acting them with movement and speech that are out of the ordinary. Ask the pupils to do the following

   - stand quite still and close their eyes

- imagine their feet are sunk firmly in the ground
- raise their arms slowly and spread them out
- puff out their cheeks
- blow as if releasing air
- keep blowing but keep their eyes closed
- open their eyes
- look at the destruction they have wreaked
- they have just created a hurricane.

2. Choose one or several pupils to be supernatural characters and stand at one end of the room. The others are 'humans' and stand or sit in the middle of the room. The supernatural characters do the above exercise of 'blowing' and the 'humans' are all blown around the room. They try to resist but cannot. They have no choice but to be blown about the room. Give as many pupils as possible the chance to be 'the wind'.

3. Now tell the children that they are all going to be the same supernatural characters who can control the weather and the elements by creating thunder, lightning and torrential rain. All pupils stand separately and spread out, then

- stand up straight and close their eyes
- concentrate
- imagine they are getting ready to create a storm
- raise their arms and bring them down with their fingertips spread wide
- every time they do this they are releasing a clap of thunder and lightning
- make their own sound effects every time they create a thunder clap.

4. Get the class into groups of five or six. One of them is to be the supernatural character and the others are humans who are on the receiving end of the bad weather conditions. After a certain amount of rehearsal the groups can perform in front of the rest of the class with a CD sound effect if possible.

5. Puck is one the most mischievous characters in the story of the play. He flies around the earth like Superman whenever he wants to, creating mayhem. Ask the children to

- smile mischievously
- get ready to fly
- and fly!

6. This time they have to learn a line from the play by heart. Puck says

> I'll put a girdle round about the earth
> In forty minutes.

Ask the children to say the line first and then fly off. Try this with them one at a time with everyone else watching. Make it a competition and choose the best Puck at the end.

7. At one point in the play Puck squeezes the juice of a flower into someone's eyes when they are asleep. Find a partner and practise the following

- the partner yawns and goes to sleep
- Puck appears and goes over
- Puck produces the flower and makes magic gestures
- Puck squeezes the flower juice into the sleeping person's eyes
- Puck disappears
- the sleeping person wakes up.

8. Both partners have to learn the following line from the play by heart

> So, awake when I am gone;
> For I must now to Oberon.

They each play the part of Puck and do the same movements as above but they have to find an appropriate point to speak the line.

Variations

- For items 1 and 2, when appropriate, play the main theme from Wagner's 'Die Walküre' to create a cataclysmic atmosphere.
- Some 'magical' music could be played for items 7 and 8. There are suitable passages from *Lord of the Rings*.

A Midsummer Night's Dream
(The Mechanicals)

In this activity we look at 'the mechanicals', who are the ordinary working characters and provide most of the comedy in the play.

Suitable for

KS1, KS2

Cross-curriculum links

English

Aims

- To represent character types clearly.
- To show awareness of comedy timing.

Resources

- A copy of A Midsummer Night's Dream

What to do

1. There are six 'mechanicals' and each has a different job. Ask the children to write a brief job description of what the following do for a living
   - a carpenter
   - a joiner
   - a weaver
   - a bellows mender
   - a tinker
   - a tailor.
2. Now ask the children to mime the above jobs. The whole class can do this together.

3. Ask them to mime the job again but adding an adjective that will make them act as a definite type of character. All the class can do the following together

- a bad-tempered carpenter
- a careful joiner
- a proud weaver
- an effeminate bellows mender
- a stupid tinker
- a handsome tailor.

4. Split the class up into groups of six. They are each to take on the following character

- Quince, the carpenter
- Snug, the joiner
- Bottom, the weaver
- Flute, the bellows mender
- Snout, the tinker
- Starveling, the tailor.

Given the descriptions in item 3, ask each character to walk into the room, one at a time, in the manner of their word description. Now ask them, in the manner of their character description, to do the following, one at a time

- enter a pub and order a drink
- walk around a supermarket doing some shopping
- go to their garage, get into their car and drive off.

5. Choose one of the locations in item 4 and tell the groups that they must all meet in that location and improvise a scene in which Quince tells them that they must all take part in an amateur play production in front of the Queen and Prince Philip!

6. Now give the groups the following lines to learn by heart. Each member of the group must speak their line according to their character description above, for example Quince will say his line in a bad-tempered way, etc.

Quince: Is all our company here?
Snug: Have you the lion's part written?

Bottom: Let me play the lion too!
Flute: Nay, faith, let me not play a woman!
Snout: You can never bring in a wall!
Starveling: I believe we must leave the killing out!

Variations

- With item 4 obviously a knowledge of one of the film versions will help the children with their characterisations.

Macbeth

> In this chapter we study an extract from Shakespeare's play *Macbeth* and learn some performance techniques.

Suitable for

KS2

Cross-curriculum links

English, History

Aims

- To research obscure words and understand their meaning.
- To speak with clarity.
- To learn about pace and rhythm in the text.

Resources

Macbeth

- An open space, either inside or outside

  (An open place
  Thunder and lightning
  Enter three WITCHES)

  Witch 1: When shall we three meet again?
  Witch 2: In thunder, lightning or in rain?
  Witch 3: When the hurlyburly's done.

  Witch 1: When the battle's lost and won.
  Witch 2: That will be ere the set of sun.
  Witch 3: Where the place?

  Witch 1: Upon the heath.
  Witch 2: There to meet with Macbeth.
  Witch 3: I come, Graymalkin.

Witch 1: Paddock calls.
Witch 2: Anon!

All: Fair is foul, and foul is fair;
Hover through the fog and filthy air.

(The witches vanish)

What to do

1. The first task is to look up the meaning of the words which are not immediately clear to the children, such as

   - hurlyburly
   - ere
   - Graymalkin
   - Paddock calls
   - anon.

2. Now that they know the meaning of the above words they can read the extract in groups of three. Those children who have the above obscure words can try the following ways of speaking them

   - stress the words
   - whisper them
   - sing them
   - shout them
   - mouth them without sound
   - break them up into syllables
   - smile as they speak the line
   - make an ugly face as they say the line
   - in a high-pitched voice
   - in a deep bass voice.

   After all these experiments the children should decide as a group which was the most effective way to say those words, and give reasons for their choice.

3. The three witches can enter in different ways before they speak any words. Try the following

   - the witches enter in slow motion
   - they enter one at a time

- they crawl in
- they jump onto the stage
- they lie on the ground and raise their heads
- they sit on the floor with their backs against a wall
- they come in and sit on one chair
- they enter as if they are blind
- they enter backwards and bump into each other
- they enter eating food.

Ask the children to decide as a group which method they prefer and why.

4. The final stage direction of this scene states that 'The witches disappear'. Find ways of making the characters disappear without using lighting. Try the following experiments

- they sink to the earth and lie quite still
- they turn their backs on the audience
- they pull black shawls over their heads and walk off
- they click their fingers and freeze
- they walk off in slow motion, backwards.

When the children have experimented with these techniques ask them to discuss them with you and others in the class and say which one they thought was the most effective.

The Cuckoo Clock (Griselda Meets Her Aunts)

In this activity we look at the first few scenes of a stage adaptation of Mrs Molesworth's *The Cuckoo Clock*. Mrs Molesworth was a popular children's writer in Victorian England. A little girl, Griselda, arrives at her aunts' home in the country.

Suitable for

KS1 (optional), KS2

Cross-curriculum link

English

Aims

- To represent different age groups.
- To show physical control.
- To understand characters through their actions.

Resources

- Extracts from *The Cuckoo Clock*, from the website

What to do

1. Tell the pupils that in the first scene Griselda arrives at an unfamiliar house and looks around curiously at everything she sees. Ask the children to imagine they have never seen the drama room (or classroom) before. Ask the class to go outside and come in again, looking around at everything as if it were totally unfamiliar to them. Then ask for volunteers to do this on their own with the rest of the class watching.

2. Now ask them to get into pairs and rehearse the following scenario. One of them is new to the school and the other knows everything about the school. Improvise a conversation in which the 'new' person asks questions about the school and the other person provides the answers. It must not be a fictional school. It must be their own school. Here are some ideas for conversations

- How long have you been here?
- What are the other children like?
- What are the teachers like?
- What is the school timetable like?
- What are the toilets like?
- Do you do much drama here?

After some rehearsal each pair can perform in front of the class.

3. Get them into groups of four and ask them to read the passage from the script in which Griselda meets the three old servants. Give the old servants a descriptor so that there is a contrast between them

- 1st servant: simple, stupid, daft, not very intelligent
- 2nd servant: snappy, bad-tempered, intolerant of children
- 3rd servant: kindly, patient, motherly, affectionate.

4. Now in pairs read the conversation between Griselda and the 3rd servant (the kindly one).

5. Ask the class to spread out and to walk about as if they were the following ages

- 2 years old
- 5 years old
- 10 years old
- 15 years old
- 20 years old
- 40 years old
- 60 years old
- 80 years old
- 100 years old.

Try starting from 100 and vice versa. Go through them quickly at first then slow down and let them focus on the age group longer. Discuss any points that arise from the children's comments.

6. Now add speech to the ages. Ask the children to say the following to each other as they are walking

- Good morning.
- I'd like a cup of tea.
- Can you tell me the way to the shops?

7. Divide the class into the different age groups, as appropriate, and ask them to move around the room according to their age and speak the lines to each other as they pass someone.

8. Now ask them to get into groups of three and read the passage from the script in which Griselda meets her aunts – Grizzell and Tabitha. Ask each group to write down an age for each character and a descriptor for each character. Discuss the conclusions with each group.

Variations

- You could play a game of 'Guess my Age'. One person at a time walks across the room and the class have to guess what age they are supposed to be by the manner in which they walk. Rather than calling out you could ask the children to write down what age is being represented. Each person reads out the number they have written down and finally the person reveals what age they intended to represent.

The Cuckoo Clock (Griselda Sees the Cuckoo Clock)

> In this activity we continue to look at the delightful story by Mrs Molesworth.

Suitable for

KS1, KS2

Cross-curriculum links

English, Art, History

Aims

- To improve timing.
- To represent inanimate objects.
- To make your own sound effects.

Resources

- A CD of sounds of a clock's ticking and chiming would be helpful

What to do

1. Ask the class to look up pictures and descriptions of cuckoos on the internet. What kind of costume would be required to play the character of the Cuckoo?

2. Discuss ways of playing the character of the Cuckoo. Then the children can make a list of ways in which the character can move and speak.

3. Give the class copies of the 'Cuckoo Chorus' speech on page 18 of the script. The whole class can read this together – one sentence each. There should be enough parts for the whole class. Get them to sit in a circle. When it's their turn they should try to make their voice different from that of the previous person to give the impression of lots of different cuckoo children speaking

- gossipy
- insulting
- argumentative
- grown-up
- babyish
- show-off.

Ask them to learn their line by heart and try it without a script!

4. Ask the class to imagine they are clocks

- all try making a ticking sound by clicking their tongues to the roof of their mouth
- they stand in a circle and someone starts ticking with one click of the tongue, then the next person does two clicks, etc.
- now they put up their hands as if they are the hour and minute hands of a clock
- all move their hands round to the appropriate time as the hour moves on.

5. Now get them into pairs and look at the conversation between the Clock and the Cuckoo. Experiment with the voice of the *Clock* by asking them to speak in the following ways

- without expression
- mechanical
- robot-like
- monotonous.

With the *Cuckoo* ask them to experiment with the following voices

- very posh
- very common
- with an accent.

6. In the same pairs ask them to improvise a conversation between two related objects

- pen and pencil
- ruler and rubber
- dustpan and brush
- clock and alarm bell.

7. Ask the children to start to write a diary entitled 'Griselda's Diary' in which she enters her thoughts on the following

- what she thinks of her two aunts
- what she thinks of the three servants
- what she thinks about the house.

Variations

- For item 4, if the children find it difficult to make the ticking sound with their tongues ask them to say 'bong' or 'bing'.
- Also with item 4, you could make it more complicated by introducing a half-hour chime or even a quarter-chime.

A Christmas Carol (Scrooge and His Nephew)

In this activity we look at the famous Christmas story by Charles Dickens in which Scrooge starts off as a mean-spirited old man who won't spend a penny more than he has to.

Suitable for

KS1, KS2

Cross·curriculum link

English

Aims

- To learn about tones of voice.

Resources

- Extracts from the website

What to do

1. Ask the children to walk about being grumpy and making grumpy-like sounds.
2. Ask them as they pass others to mutter 'humbug, Christmas is humbug'.
3. Ask them to say the following lines to each other in a really sarcastic tone of voice
   - Charitable? Pleasant time?
   - What things? What good?
   - Because you fell in love!
   - Who in God's name are you?

- Are there no prisons?
- And the union workhouses? Are they still in operation?
- You mean money?

4. Now as they walk around ask them to say the following lines to each other in a very strong tone of voice

  - Keep your head down over your books!
  - Get on with your work!
  - I wish to be left alone!
  - Then let them die!
  - Get out!

5. Tell them that that was the sound of Scrooge talking. He is sarcastic, mean and a bully. That is the tone of voice he adopts in the scenes they are about to read. Now, however, we are going to use the tone of voice of Fred, Scrooge's nephew. Fred is kindly, expansive and friendly. They should walk about, stop and say the following lines to people as they pass them

  - A Merry Christmas, God save you!
  - God bless Christmas!
  - Why cannot we be friends?
  - Well, God bless you!
  - Give my kindest regards to all your family.
  - And a Happy New Year.

6. Now ask them to get into pairs and choose a couple of lines from the above selection. One of them chooses lines for Fred, the other chooses lines for Scrooge. Ask them to walk about and say the lines to each other repeatedly. They must each maintain the correct tone of voice for the character.

7. Now in their pairs ask them to read the first scene of the script between Fred, the nephew, and Scrooge. They will now have some idea of the tone of voice to adopt for the two characters.

Scrooge will be

  - gruff
  - mean
  - humourless
  - emotionless
  - hard.

Fred will be

- cheerful
- generous
- forgiving
- warm
- hearty.

8. Ask the class to study the following words and phrases and make sure they know what they mean and how to pronounce them

- dismal
- morose
- balancing your books and having every item in 'em
- through a round dozen of months
- presented dead against you
- charitable
- by losing your situation
- I wonder you don't go into Parliament
- resolute.

9. Now they should read the scene again and try to make an even stronger contrast between the tone of voice of the two characters.

A Christmas Carol (Scrooge and the Charity Collectors)

In this activity we deal with the scene in which Scrooge flatly refuses to give money to charity.

Suitable for

KS1 (optional), KS2

Cross-curriculum links

English, History

Aims

- To improve character interpretation through voice.
- To use variations of tone.

Resources

- Charity collecting tins
- Toy money, coins and notes

What to do

1. Divide the class up into charity collectors and members of the public. Give all the charity collectors a tin each and ask them to stand still in a part of the room. They must call out the name of their 'charity organisation' and ask for a donation from the rest of the class. For example

   - 'Save the Children', please give generously to 'Save the Children'
   - 'Doctor Barnardo's', please give generously for orphan children.

   The children who are members of the public walk about the room and are attracted or not by the various 'callings out' and give (or not) according to how they feel. Supply them if possible with toy money or they will have to mime.

2. Select one of the class to be Scrooge. While everybody else gives generously Scrooge walks about and gives nothing. The class can get together to talk about Scrooge and how mean he is.

3. Select a group of three people to be charity collectors. All three are happy and smiling. They walk about with smiles on their faces and ask for money. Everybody gives generously – except for the person selected to be Scrooge! The class get together and discuss why Mr Scrooge never gives anything.

4. Before getting into groups to read the 'charitables' scene ask the class to look up and/or discuss the following words and phrases

- mission of mercy
- you are absolved, my son
- liberality
- destitute
- common necessities
- common comforts
- union workhouses (cross-curricular – History)
- the treadmill and the Poor Law (cross-curricular – History)
- the multitude
- want is keenly felt by many
- anonymous
- decrease the surplus population
- well, we never!

5. Get the class into groups of four to have a first reading of the 'charitables' scene from the script. Give descriptors to the three charitables so that they form a contrast to each other

- no. 1 – pious, sonorous, deep tones
- no. 2 – bustling busybody, do-gooder
- no. 3 – angry working-class type.

6. Ask the three charitables to practise saying the following in unison

- You are absolved, my son. God forgives you!
- We are going in!
- We do not understand, sir!
- Mr Scrooge!
- Well, we never!

7. Get them all to write an entry in their diary, as one of the charitable gentlemen, in which they describe what happened when they called at Scrooge and Marley.

8. Ask the children to join another group of three and improvise a scene in which they tell each other what happened when they called at Scrooge and Marley.

Variations

- As a piece of pre-lesson research you could ask the children to do some research into charities so that they will have an idea of what they are going to be collecting for.
- It would also be appropriate for the children to do a little cross-curricular History research into Victorian workhouses and the Poor Laws of the time.

A Christmas Carol (*Scrooge* and Cratchit)

In this activity we look at the relationship between Scrooge and Bob Cratchit, which is a relationship between bully and victim.

Suitable for

KS1, KS2

Cross-curriculum link

English

Aims

- To convey contrasting physical types.
- To convey vocal contrast.

Resources

- Extracts from the website

What to do

1. Divide the class into two. One half are 'Scrooge bullies' and the other half are 'Cratchit victims'. Separate the two groups to different sides of the room.

Ask the 'Scrooges'

- to get into an aggressive frozen pose

and the 'Cratchits'

- to get into a defensive frozen pose.

2. Tell them that you are going to clap your hands (or beat a drum) and on each beat the children must suddenly change their frozen pose into another aggressive or defensive frozen pose. This can be quite melodramatic.

3. Pair up the children and do the same as in item 2. Do at least ten frozen poses. After they have got used to it, each pair can be watched by the rest of the class.

4. Now tell them that they are, in their pairs, going to do consecutive frozen action but divided into about ten freeze frames. For example Scrooge is going to

- come into the room
- see that Cratchit has put a lump of coal on the fire
- scream at him
- Cratchit gets up
- moves to the fireplace
- takes out the coal
- burns his hand
- Scrooge looks on in horror
- Cratchit drops the coal on the floor
- Scrooge rages at him
- Cratchit is in pain
- Scrooge orders him out!

5. In pairs they read the scene between Scrooge and Cratchit starting at 'You'll want all day off tomorrow, I suppose?' They should try to provide a vocal contrast between Scrooge and Cratchit.

Cratchit's voice is

- submissive
- whiney
- respectful
- apologetic
- hesitant.

Scrooge's voice is

- sharp
- brisk
- insistent
- unfeeling
- bad-tempered.

Remind them to incorporate everything they've learnt about aggressive and submissive postures from the previous exercises.

6. Now ask the children to look at the exchange between Scrooge and Cratchit right at the end of the play. Scrooge has had his 'conversion' and is now only pretending to be angry with Cratchit. Ask the pairs to rehearse the scene with Scrooge as his former self, with his former aggressive tone, and then suddenly change so that Cratchit is quite bewildered when Scrooge says, 'I am going to raise your salary'.

As a lead-up to the scene ask the class to rehearse reacting to the following announcements

- you've won the lottery
- you've passed your exams
- no school tomorrow.

Now the pairs can read the scene between Scrooge and Cratchit.

7. Ask the children to write a note from Cratchit to Scrooge asking for Christmas Day off because he is too scared to ask him face to face.

Variations

- With item 4 the children can make up their own scenario as long as it is Scrooge bullying Cratchit in some way.

A Christmas Carol (Unearthly Characters)

In this activity we look at ways of presenting unearthly characters based on the three 'ghosts' from the script of *A Christmas Carol*.

Suitable for

KS1, KS2

Cross-curriculum links

English, History

Aims

- To learn not to laugh.
- To learn to focus the concentration.

Resources

- A CD of spooky violin music
- A book

What to do

1. Ask the class to spread out and stand quite still. You are going to move amongst the class and anyone who moves a muscle or laughs is going to be 'out' and must sit down. The aim is to be as still as possible. The last person left standing is the winner.

2. Now ask them to get into a pose that they think of as being that of a ghost or of an unearthly creature. Again walk amongst the class and anyone who moves or laughs is 'out'.

3. Now tell them that you are going to ask them two questions, the same two questions that Scrooge asks the first ghost in *A Christmas Carol*

   1st question: Are you a spirit?
   2nd question: Are you the spirit whose coming was foretold me?

To both questions the class, all together, must reply 'I am'. Anyone who laughs is out and must sit down.

4. Now you go up to each person in the class and ask the same questions of each individual, who must reply 'I am'. Tell them that you are looking to cast the part of 'The Ghost of Christmas Past'. Anyone who laughs will, of course, ruin their chances!

5. Tell the class that the part of 'The Ghost of Christmas Past' is meant to be played by a child so that they do not need to put on a spooky voice or anything like that. Put them into pairs and ask them to read the dialogue between Scrooge and 'Christmas Past'.

6. Ask the pairs to practise moving in slow motion together from the point where 'Christmas Past' says 'Rise and walk with me'. They can practise moving in slow motion (without scripts) in the following ways

   - Scrooge stands and they move together in a full circle in the same direction
   - Scrooge stands and they turn 360 degrees, standing on the spot
   - Scrooge stands and they move in a circle but in opposite directions
   - Scrooge stands and they move forwards, then left, then right.

   A suitable piece of spooky violin music would be very atmospheric to use for this part of the lesson, such as Rachmaninov's 'Isle of the Dead'.

7. In their pairs ask them to practise looking in the same direction when 'Christmas Past' says 'Look there'. Ask them to fix their eyes on the same spot in the distance.

8. In groups of three add the character of 'Child Scrooge'. The smallest person in the group should ideally be 'Child Scrooge'. They practise reading the lines. Make sure that 'Child Scrooge' is at a distance from the other two. 'Child Scrooge' should be carrying a book.

9. As a part of English and/or History lessons the children should research the following in order to understand fully the references to the books that Scrooge read as a child

   - the story of Ali Baba
   - Robinson Crusoe.

Dracula (part 1)

> This activity features an extract from Michael Theodorou's stage adaptation of Bram Stoker's novel *Dracula*. The extract can be copied and used for the various activities indicated in this chapter and the next.

Suitable for

KS2

Cross-curriculum link

English

Aims

- To read in a group.
- How to use pause for dramatic effect.

Resources

- Copies of the extract from *Dracula*

Extract from *Dracula*

Characters
Professor Van Helsing
Jonathan
Arthur
Jayne

THE CELLARS OF CARFAX ABBEY
(*A dark, empty space with a vaulted ceiling where Dracula has been in hiding. Enter Professor Van Helsing, Jonathan, Arthur and Jayne all carrying lamps. They peer around trying to make out shapes in the darkness. The lamps cast huge shadows over the walls and ceilings. When they speak there is a cavernous echo that makes their voices sound unreal.*)

VAN HELSING
You know this place, Jonathan, you have copied maps of it. Which is the way to the chapel?

JONATHAN
Through here, I think.

ARTHUR
My God, the stench!

JAYNE
Foul. It's unbearable.

VAN HELSING
Through here, this is the chapel.
Can you feel it?
Can you feel his presence?

JONATHAN
Yes, he is here.
But where?

ARTHUR (*suddenly*)
Quiet!
(*They all listen with apprehension, huddling together as if for protection.*)

JAYNE
Can you hear it?
(*A strange, eerie sound like a hum is heard.*)

VAN HELSING
Stay together, back to back. Do not move.
(*They stand together in a circle back to back.*)

JAYNE
What is it?

VAN HELSING
Stay still!
(*The hum increases in volume.*)

JONATHAN (*pointing*)
Professor, he's there!

ARTHUR
Quickly, he's out there!
Bring all the lamps!
Quickly!
(*They all rush out.*)

What to do

1. Get the class into groups of four and give each group copies of the script. Ask them to allocate parts to the group and then start reading it aloud.

2. After each group has finished reading the whole extract at least twice, ask each group to get into a frozen picture for the following lines from the script

   - My God, the stench!
   - Can you feel his presence?
   - Quiet!
   - Stay together, back to back.

3. Ask all the class to stand together and make the following sound effects

   - the sound of an eerie hum
   - dripping water
   - whistling wind
   - a ghostly wail
   - frogs croaking
   - deep breathing
   - insane laughter.

Dracula (part 2)

The activities in this session centre around an episode from Michael Theodorou's dramatisation of the Bram Stoker novel *Dracula*. As you have discovered from the last chapter there are four characters searching an old, dank cellar for evidence of the evil Dracula's presence.

Suitable for

KS2

Cross-curriculum links

English, History, Geography

Aims

- To work together as a team.
- To create suspense through performance techniques.
- To create atmosphere through sound and lighting.

Resources

- a microphone with amplification (optional)
- cloaks, gloves, hats
- lamps or torches to be used as props
- a map of Europe

What to do

1. Arrange the class into groups of four and ask them to carry out the following tasks

   - hold hands and walk very slowly and silently
   - stand back to back looking around as if surrounded by an unknown force

- creep along the floor together
- shake hands with each other as if wishing good luck
- stand in a line and all look one way then another
- each raise your right hand and swear an oath that you will work together against evil
- look up and point together at the same object
- hold hands because you are afraid.

2. Now ask the groups to repeat the previous activities but this time they must add words to their actions. Allow each group to rehearse then perform their extract in front of the rest of the class.

3. One person from each group must be selected to be 'invisible'. The 'invisible' person stands outside the group. The rest of the group start looking for him but, as he is invisible, they cannot see him anywhere. The 'invisible' person then claps his hands. The group immediately look in his direction but the 'invisible' person moves elsewhere and they look in vain for him. It is important to stress to the children that for the purposes of this exercise the group must not see the 'invisible' person or even pretend to. The group must get more and more frustrated as they hear noises but cannot see anything.

Try the following noises for the 'invisible' person to make

- click of fingers
- tap on a chair or a wall
- bang on the floor
- close of a door
- a cackle of laughter.

Each member of the group can have a go at being the 'invisible' person. Towards the end of the session each group of four can present their best work to the others.

4. Now ask each group to sit together and shut their eyes while making a humming sound. The humming sound should be tried in the following ways

- starting quietly and increasing in volume
- starting loudly and decreasing to silence
- starting and stopping suddenly
- starting then stopping then starting again.

It is important that the children shut their eyes and concentrate, listening to each other so that they are all making the same sound.

5. Look at a map of Europe to locate Transylvania. This is where 'Dracula' lives in his castle. Now find London. With your help ask the children to plot a route from Transylvania to England, noting which countries they have to pass through and the important towns or cities through which they may have to pass. Remind them that they may have to cross water as well as land! When the class as a whole has agreed on a route, choose people from the class to be specific countries or towns and stand around the studio or classroom. You can, if you wish, make country signs to be held above the head.

Select a member of the class to be 'Dracula'. The mode of transport will be a stagecoach drawn by a team of four horses. Choose four members of the class to be the horses. There may also be a boat or ship to transport 'Dracula' at various stages of his journey. Choose people to be the ship and the captain of the ship with possibly some passengers. When all this has been decided and the casting has been agreed 'Dracula' must make the journey from Transylvania to London.

6. The final part of this session is to work on the script from *Dracula*. Give each member of the class a script and ask them to get into groups of four. They can either choose their own roles or you can allocate parts to them. There are four characters in the scene and each has a different personality

- VAN HELSING is old but strong-willed
- JONATHAN is impulsive and young
- ARTHUR is aristocratic and has a posh accent
- JAYNE is brainy with glasses.

You could suggest that, as a starting point, before reading the script, each person in the group stands up and speaks the following lines in an appropriate voice

- I am Van Helsing and I am…
- I am Jonathan and I am…
- I am Arthur and I am…
- I am Jayne and I am…

Other characteristics can be found, of course, as the children become more familiar with the script and it certainly does not matter if girls play the boy parts.

Ask the children to rehearse and to try to convey an atmosphere of

- fear
- dread
- apprehension
- suspense
- menace.

Finally, each group can perform their piece in front of the class or they can learn their lines for homework and perform on another day. The final performances could be enhanced by lighting and sound effects.

Variations

- For item 6 someone from another group can play the role of 'Dracula'.

Great Expectations (The Convict)

In this activity we look at the opening scene of the book by Charles Dickens in which Pip is confronted by a sinister character.

Suitable for

KS2

Cross-curriculum links

History, Art, English

Aims

- To extend vocabulary.
- To represent objects in a realistic manner.

Resources

- A lantern with a blue gel (optional)
- Sound effects of the wind blowing (optional)
- Black material or cloaks
- A bunch of flowers
- The DVD of *Great Expectations*

What to do

1. As a part of History lessons the children should do some research into Victorian prisons and prisoners. Select some images from the internet of what prisoners used to wear so that if a stage production were attempted they would know what kind of costume the convict would be wearing.

2. As a part of their English lessons the children should look up the meaning of the following words and phrases from the opening scene

so that when they speak the lines they are aware of exactly what the words mean

- convict
- give it mouth
- ravenously
- late of this Parish
- blacksmith
- file
- wittles.

3. It would probably be best to show the class the first 15 minutes of the DVD of *Great Expectations* before proceeding to the practical work.

4. Tell the class to get into groups of three or four. Each group represents a tombstone in a churchyard. One of the class is chosen to be the sinister convict hiding behind a tombstone. Another person is chosen to be Pip and has to leave the room. When Pip is out of the room the Convict hides behind a group of tombstones and Pip is invited to come back into the room. The game can be played in the following ways

- Pip is only allowed to take two steps into the room and then has to guess where the Convict is hidden.
- Pip is only allowed to take two steps into the room and is only given ten seconds to guess.
- Pip turns his/her back on the class and the Convict changes position. Pip then has to guess again.
- If Pip guesses correctly he has another go, if not, another person becomes Pip.

5. Two children are designated to be the tombstones of Pip's mother and father, standing side by side. The rest of the class represent other tombstones. A person is selected to be Pip who must enter and lay a wreath of flowers at his parents' tombstones. The 'Convict' will have already been hidden behind one of the tombstones and jumps out to scare Pip. If the lights could be turned down a little the effect of eeriness could be achieved.

6. Get the class into pairs and ask them to read the script with the following vocal descriptors to help them

- the Convict – a rough voice possibly with an accent or dialect
- Pip – fearful and blurting out answers quickly.

7. Get the class back together again and select two people to be Pip and the Convict. The class as a whole could rehearse in the following ways

- the rest of the class could be tombstones and trees and make the sound of the wind blowing
- the tombstones could echo the Convict's voice in a whisper
- the tombstones could slowly rise and fall in a sinister fashion using black cloaks or black material.

Variations

- The process in item 4 can be speeded up by Pip just turning his/her back while the Convict hides.

Great Expectations (The Tickler)

> In this activity we look at the next episode from *Great Expectations* when Pip returns home late after meeting the Convict in the churchyard.

Suitable for

KS2

Cross-curriculum link

English

Aims

- To understand themes from text.
- To use themes to create character.

Resources

- The DVD of *Great Expectations*
- Sound effect of cannon fire

What to do

1. Ask the children to write down as many reasons as possible for being late for school, for example the bus was late, or I fell over and hurt my leg.

2. Discuss the various reasons they have written down and then in pairs ask them to improvise a scene between a teacher and a pupil. The pupil is late for school and must give an excuse which the teacher may or may not accept.

3. Now ask them to write down reasons for being late arriving home.

4. Discuss the various reasons they have written and then put them into pairs to improvise a scene between a parent – either mum or dad – and a child. The child is late home and must give a reason for being late.

5. Review some of the dialogues and ask any of the pairs if they wish to perform them in front of the class. Discuss the differences between being late for school and being late home.

6. Put the children into groups of three. Give them the situation in which a child is late home and mum and dad are getting really worried. The child eventually turns up.

7. Still in their groups of three ask them to make the mum a really domineering character who henpecks the husband and is always bossing him about. The child is late again and mum has been out searching for him/her. Let us see what happens when the child turns up.

8. Again, if there are any groups that wish to perform their dialogues in front of the whole class, let them.

9. Now give out the script of 'The Tickler' from *Great Expectations* and ask them to read it in the same groups of three if possible. Tell them that the husband, Joe, is henpecked by Mrs Joe who is a very fearsome character.

10. As a part of their English lessons ask them to write a diary in which Pip recounts his adventure of meeting the Convict in the churchyard and returning home to be thrashed by Mrs Joe.

Great Expectations (Stealing the Pie)

In this activity we look at the internal anguish that Pip goes through and the guilt that he feels when he steals food and drink from his home to take to the Convict.

Suitable for

KS2

Cross-curriculum link

English

Aims

- To learn to play inanimate objects.
- To learn to play unrealistic characters.
- To learn to play animals.
- To increase the power of imagination.

Resources

- Extract from *Great Expectations* on the website

What to do

1. Show them the section of the DVD of *Great Expectations* (the David Lean version) when Pip gets up at night to steal the pie.

2. Get the class into groups of three and give them the following roles

   - a young person
   - the good conscience
   - the evil spirit.

   Ask the groups to decide on something that the person will steal. The unrealistic characters of the 'good conscience' and the 'evil spirit' accompany the person and speak to him/her but cannot touch them

- the 'good conscience' tries to persuade *not* to steal
- the 'evil' spirit' tries to persuade to steal.

Try to suggest two different voices for the 'consciences'

- a pious, religious voice for the 'good conscience'
- a gangster voice for the 'evil spirit'.

3. In the same groups of three they act out the following scenario but the 'consciences' have to whisper

> Pip is lying down in bed with the two consciences standing over him. Pip slowly gets up and tiptoes down the stairs. The consciences follow, whispering the following.
>
> 'Stop, thief!'
>
> 'Get up Mrs Joe.'
>
> Pip opens the pantry door.
>
> The two consciences vie for his attention as he steals the following items
>
> bread
> cheese
> mincemeat
> brandy
> pie.
>
> Pip leaves the house.

4. Read to the children or photocopy the following extract from the novel

> The gates and dykes and banks came bursting at me through the mist, as if they cried as plainly as could be, 'A boy with somebody else's pork pie! Stop him!' The cattle came upon me with like suddenness, staring out of their eyes, and steaming out of their nostrils, 'Hello, young thief!' One black ox with a white cravat on – who even had to my awakened conscience something of a clerical air – fixed me so obstinately with his eyes, and moved his blunt head round in such an accusatory manner as I moved round, that I blubbered out to him 'I couldn't help it, sir! It wasn't for myself I took it.'

5. Get the class into large groups of six or seven characters as follows

- gate
- dyke
- bank

- cattle
- black ox
- Pip.

Ask the groups to become the inanimate objects and the animals. They have become, in Pip's imagination, like real people accusing him of stealing. As Pip passes through they all say something to him to accuse him.

6. As a part of an English lesson the whole passage can be read from the novel, starting at the end of Chapter 2 and continuing into Chapter 3 when Pip arrives at the churchyard to give the Convict his food.

7. Also as part of English lessons, continue Pip's diary to include the stealing of the pie and the morning journey to the graveyard.

Variations

- Item 5 could be filmed if a video camera is available at your school.

Goodbye, Mr Chips (Teacher's Nightmare)

In this final activity we look at a scene from the film of *Goodbye, Mr Chips* in which a schoolmaster is mercilessly taunted and plagued by a class of malevolent pupils.

Suitable for

KS1 (optional), KS2

Cross-curriculum link

English

Aims

- To show physical representation of character types.
- To show how to put scenes into a sequence.
- To revisit dramatic pause.

Resources

- DVD of the film version of *Goodbye, Mr Chips* starring Robert Donat
- A schoolmaster's mortar board or any other kind of hat that is appropriate to throw around
- Pieces of scrunched up paper that can be thrown around

What to do

1. Show the class the black and white film version of *Goodbye, Mr Chips* starring Robert Donat as the unfortunate schoolmaster, Mr Chipping. The first twenty minutes should be enough. Ask them to focus especially on the scene in which Mr Chipping takes the 'prep' class that ends in a riot.

2. The class are going to concentrate on the character of a schoolmaster or schoolmistress 'of the old school'. Ask them to spread out and find frozen poses for the following

- an old teacher
- a young teacher
- a strict teacher
- a short-sighted teacher
- a PE teacher
- an art teacher
- a maths teacher
- a science teacher
- a head teacher
- any teacher you know.

3. Now ask the class to add voice to their characterisation. Repeat the above list and ask the children to speak as the teacher. This can be done all together or one by one.

4. Ask the class to get into pairs. One is a 'good' pupil, the other is a 'naughty' pupil. Ask them to compose three frozen photographs in which

- one pupil is being naughty and the other looks on in horror.

Then ask them to show their three versions by saying

- photograph 1
- photograph 2
- photograph 3.

5. Get them into groups of eight and ask them to be teachers in a staff room. They must improvise a scene based on the film in which the new teacher is introduced by the head teacher. They warn him/her about the dreadful class. Casting will be as follows

- head teacher
- new teacher
- six other teachers.

For the six other teachers try to create a 'character' from the list in item 2.

6. In the same groups of eight ask them to improvise a scene in which pupils are waiting for the 'new teacher' to arrive. Ask them to have a mixture of good pupils and naughty pupils. The following ideas for dialogue could be used

- Has anyone seen him/her?
- What's he/she like?
- Shall we play a trick on him/her?
- What if the head teacher comes in?
- Who's got ideas for tricks?

The scene ends when one of them says 'Quiet, here he/she comes!'

7. Tell them that the entrance of the head teacher is a perfect example of '*dramatic pause*'.

Still in their groups of eight ask one of them to be the head teacher. The rest must practise making as much noise as possible and then 'see' the head teacher. The dramatic pause is the silence that follows. Get the groups to perform this, one group at a time, with the other groups watching.

8. Now give them copies of the script adapted from the film and ask them to read it through. They should be able to rehearse and cast the parts themselves and rehearse to performance level – if lines can be learnt.

9. As a part of English lessons the teacher can recount in diary form his/her unpleasant experience with the naughty class.

Variations

- With item 7, the groups watching can add to the noise but they must fall silent as soon as the head teacher enters.

Appendix

Suggested music for drama sessions

1. For years I used a piece of music called 'Aerobic Exercise Music', which contains a variety of fast speeds and was excellent for warm-ups, movement exercises and animal work, and served as a bckground to comedy mime work.

   There is a website called **www.altered-state.com** that contains a healthy variety of New Age Music.

2. Another helpful site for exploring suitable music, especially for slow motion work and group movement, is **www.aeoliah.com**.

3. Another useful site for relaxation music and uplifting music for movement work is **www.newworldmusic.com**. You can also listen to samples on this site without paying.

4. Saint-Saëns 'The Carnival of the Animals' is essential for some of the chapters on animal movement

   Track 4: Tortoises
   Track 6: Kangaroos
   Track 7: The Aquarium (Fish)
   Track 9: Cuckoo in the Heart of the Woods
   Track 10: The Aviary (Birds)
   Track 13: The Swan.

5. For fast and furious movement and for Melodrama, witches, etc., Bela Bartok's opening to 'The Miraculous Mandarin' is very stimulating.

6. For any poetic mood music, either for actual movement or as a stimulus to imaginative visualisation, Shostakovich's 'Suite from the film *The Gadfly*' is perfect, especially track 4, 'Interlude' and track 8, 'Romance'.

7. 'The Planets' by Holst provides a good range of music to use in class, especially 'Mars' for strongly dramatic movement and 'Neptune' for anything involving slower movement of an unrealistic nature.

8. An unusual and very stimulating piece of music is 'Utrenja' by Penderecki, especially track 2, 'Velicanija', which is perfect for unearthly sounds and background music, or could be used for movement when children are enacting aliens, etc.

9. Rimsky Korsakov's 'Scheherazade' is very useful, especially the episodes of 'The Sea' and 'The Shipwreck' for lively group movement work, pirate fights, etc.

10. 'Peter and the Wolf' by Prokofiev is a great piece of music for movement and text for speaking and enacting both animals and humans.

11. Rachmaninov's 'The Isle of the Dead' is a very hypnotic and atmospheric piece of music that could be used on any occasion when slow repetitive movement is required.

12. For highly dramatic effects and big movement work I would suggest the opening of Carl Orff's 'Carmina Burana' 'O Fortuna'.

13. John Philip Sousa's 'Liberty Bell March' is a good example of military-style music.

Suggested film DVDs

Some of these are referred to in various chapters of the book and others are recommendations for quality viewing by children.

1. *Great Expectations* (1946) directed by David Lean.

2. *Oliver* (1948) directed by David Lean.

3. *A Kid for Two Farthings* (1955), a young boy growing up in the East End of London meets a 'unicorn', directed by Carol Reed.

4. *Goodbye, Mr Chips* (1939), set in a boys' school at the end of the nineteenth century and moving into the early twentieth century, starring Robert Donat.

5. There are many versions of *The Secret Garden* but probably one of the best and most authentic is the BBC TV series (1975), which can be obtained now on DVD, starring Sarah Hollis Andrews, John Woodnut and Hope Johnstone.

6. *A Little Princess* (1996) based on the novel by Frances Hodgson Burnett, with Liesel Matthews.

7. *The Red Balloon* (1956) features a six-year-old boy and his best friend, a balloon that bops along with him to school and protects him from bullies. A classic film with Pascal Lamorisse.

8. *A Midsummer Night's Dream* (1996) with Lindsay Duncan.

9. *ET: The Extra Terrestrial* (1982) with Henry Thomas, Robert Macnaughton and Dee Wallace.

10. *Babe* (1995), a wonderful fantasy based on Dick King-Smith's novel *The Sheep-Pig*.

11. *Mary Poppins* (1964) with Julie Andrews.

12. *A Tree Grows in Brooklyn* (1945), a wonderful film about a creative girl on the teeming streets of tenement Brooklyn, New York.

13. *The Wizard of Oz* (1939), the classic children's film with Judy Garland.

14. *Superman* (1978), still the best version ever of this classic story, with Christopher Reeve.

15. *Bugsy Malone* (1976), Alan Parker's mini-mobster musical with Jodie Foster.

16. *It's a Wonderful Life* (1946), a truly moving evocation of family life with James Stewart, directed by Frank Capra.

17. *A Christmas Carol* (1999) with Patrick Stewart as Scrooge.

18. *Peter Pan* (2003) with Jason Isaacs and Jeremy Sumpter or (1956) with Mary Martin.

19. *My Fair Lady* (1964) with Julie Andrews.

20. *The Sound of Music* (1965) with Julie Andrews.

Suggested props for classroom use

I have always found the following useful to have in my props cupboard. A quick visit to the local charity shop will yield most items listed below.

1. A variety of canes and walking sticks
2. Hats of various kinds and sizes
3. Scarves and gloves
4. Spectacle frames
5. Plastic plates, cups, beakers, etc.
6. Shawls
7. Blankets
8. Pens, pencils, rulers, rubbers, old books or ledgers
9. Toy paper money and plastic coins
10. Sunglasses
11. Cloaks of various colours, especially black
12. Teacloths, tablecloths, place settings
13. Plastic pot plants and plastic flowers
14. Face masks
15. Tea cosies

16. A selection of Christmas decorations
17. Hair ribbons, hair grips, hair nets
18. Aprons
19. Doilies
20. Handkerchiefs
21. Elastic bands
22. Packs of playing cards
23. Tennis balls, small balls, beach ball
24. Brooms, mops, dustpans and brushes, plastic buckets
25. Old keys
26. Wrap-around, long black skirts
27. Bells, chimes, whistles, rattles
28. Free-standing clock
29. Wigs
30. Neckties
31. Bandanas
32. Dolls, teddy bears, stuffed animals
33. Pair of dice
34. Handbags of assorted sizes
35. Rope
36. Umbrellas
37. Spyglass, telescope, binoculars
38. Paper dipped in tea for old scrolls
39. Toy drum or a recorder
40. A triangle (musical instrument)
41. Two short pieces of wood for banging together to create sound effects of different kinds
42. Telephones – the old-fashioned variety or mobiles